INTRODUCTION

Joan Rimmer is a Warrington Magi journalist and a Manager and controlled "Community Home with Education", Newton-le- The school stands on the site of the former Liverpool Farm School, and it was while browsing through some old books and documents there that she first became interested in the work of the Liverpool Juvenile Reformatory Association, founded in 1855. Today the interests of the Association are represented by twenty Trustee Managers, four of whom are on the Board of Managers of the present school, together with eight representatives of the County Council Social Services Committee.

In this book Mrs Rimmer traces the work of the three main branches of the Association - the industrial training ship Akbar, the two girls' reformatories at Mount Vernon Green and Toxteth·

The unhappy faces of these street urchins illustrate their despair. For many such children, to be picked up later in their childhood for a misdemeanour or vagrancy, the reformatory system offered a chance of a stable future and respectability

Park, and the Liverpool Farm School, which was originally founded to cater for boys not strong enough to withstand the rigours of life on the Akbar. She has drawn extensively on the minute books, annual reports, punishment books and letters of the Association dating back to the year of foundation, and a selection of Superintendents' letters is included. To complete the picture, there is a brief account of the Roman Catholic reformatory ship Clarence, and a chapter tracing the history of offences and punishment from Victorian days to the penalties imposed at Heswall Nautical School in the 1950s.

It is an absorbing and wide-ranging study. The details of daily routine, diet and health, rebellion and its aftermath, success and rewards, and the administrative problems of economy and after-care are all there, but beyond this Mrs Rimmer writes with a sympathy which brings out vividly the personalities of some of the officers and children involved. There are fascinating insights into Victorian social conditions and attitudes, and the book raises some challenging questions about the effects (good and bad) of the gradual change in those attitudes on society today.

Joan Rimmer has also written "The Years of Transition and Red Bank Today", bringing the reformatory story up to date. It is available priced £1 from Red Bank School, Newton-le-Willows, Merseyside WA12 8EA

Acknowledgements

I should like to thank the following people and organisations for their generosity in providing illustrations for this book: Commander Martin Johnson, GM, RNR (retired), the last Captain of the Heswall Nautical School, formerly the Akbar. The Cheshire Police Museum, Crewe; Miss B E Frann, Director, Catholic Social Services, Arch Diocese of Liverpool; Mr T Welch, General Manager, St Thomas More Centre, Birkdale; Mr Frank Boden, Warrington Photographic Society; T Edmanson (Photographic Services), Lowton, Warrington; Ian Southerin (Photographic Services), New Ferry, Birkenhead; Mr L Jackson, Red Bank School; Mr Rodney Heathcote (Photographic Services); Mr Frank Heaton.

Akbar boys, around 1890

From "The Liverpool Mercury," Thursday 25th December 1879:

"The well-established fact that 75 percent of the Reformatory children who pass through these places of homely correction and instruction do well in their subsequent career, lifts the good cause entirely out of the region of doubt and despair.

Considering the strange enigmas of humanity with which they deal - the terrible familiarity with wickedness and precocity in the criminal spirit - the 75 percent becomes, indeed, one of the greatest facts of our attempt at social reform. Cardinal Wiseman it was, we think, who, many years ago, said he could make anything of a child given into his care at six or eight years of age. But the downward education of a street arab, in most cases, begins almost in infancy. He inherits the fearful craving for drink bequeathed by a besotted mother or father and, too often, has besides, a natural predisposition for that form of crime which in the higher walks of life is called Kleptomania, and which phrenologists account for by an abnormal development of the bump of acquisitiveness.

Inherited taints of character and an education in squalid poverty and brutal degradation commences with the first dawning of individualism. All the fates appear to be against the child becoming anything else but a criminal."

IDEAS OF REFORM

Thursday 11th January, 1855, dawned in a flurry of snowflakes. A bitter east wind gusted in from the River Mersey and in many of Liverpool's 14,000 dark inhabited cellars the pools of muddy stagnant water which puddled the floors were glazed with black ice.

In the Magistrates' Room in the Sessions House, a group of important be-whiskered gentlemen removed their top hats and overcoats, gratefully defrosted their frigid lungs in the warmth radiating from the blazing hearth and, after toasting their extremities in the rosy glow, settled down to the business of the day - an idea which, in fulfilment, was to change the course of destiny for many thousands of criminal and destitute gutter children.

In the chair was His Worship the Mayor, John Stewart, presiding over a company which included one Member of Parliament, two gentlemen of the cloth and fourteen ship owners and merchants. They were, in the main, bountiful of fortune and influence, enjoying the comforts and privileges of the prosperous and occupying elegant mansions with panoramic views of the riverside scene.

It was a world remote from the wretched existence eked out by the poor in the heart of the city, less than a mile away. Here thousands of homeless and neglected children, barefoot and ragged, haunted the alleys like flickering shadows, sleeping rough in doorways, their stomachs aching with perpetual hunger.

There was no joy in childhood for these street urchins. Coming from indifferent and poverty-enmeshed stock, they relied on their wits, crime and prostitution for survival; those who lacked initiative died.

Prisons tenanted by the very young were a saddening sight. In 1850 there were 15,000 juvenile lawbreakers or vagrants sharing cells with hardened criminals, under whose expert guidance they soon developed whatever felonious tendencies they possessed, to emerge as fully-fledged villains.

It was an area of great concern and challenge for those with a social conscience. Around the mahogany table in the Magistrates' Room that grey January day sat gentlemen who were convinced, like other reformers of the period, that with proper help and guidance youthful offenders could be transformed into decent and virtuous citizens. An attempt must be made to combine some education with the discipline of the prison itself, and punishment for evil doing blended with instruction.

It was the Government's Youthful Offenders' Act of 1854, which recognised law breakers under the age of 16 as a separate group, that really paved the way for benevolent groups of people throughout the country to put their philanthropic theories into practice. The Act, "For the Better Care and Reformation of Youthful Offenders in Great Britain," gave the courts authority to send anyone under 16 to a reformatory school at the end of any prison sentence of at least 14 days duration.

For the Liverpool gentlemen this Act was an opportunity to be grasped. It was proposed by William Rathbone, Esq, seconded by T D Anderson, Esq, and formally resolved that a Committee be formed for the purpose of establishing on Merseyside three Reformatories, two for boys and one for girls. The children could expect hard labour, hard fare and a hard bed; treatment must be fair and discipline strict but directed mainly towards deterrence. So might moral reformation come through the tempering of punishment. The children would be educated to a reasonable standard, given an industrial training and taught that there was "A God, a heaven and a hell."

For many thousands this was to be their only chance of a stable future, and for some an almost magical opportunity to rise to positions of importance and respectability. Such boys became Masters of their own vessels, prosperous businessmen and war heroes. In the New World across the Atlantic they achieved ambitions and fulfilled aspirations which had hitherto been daydreams of impossible magnitude. The girls "married very respectably," which in those far away days was the zenith of every girl's ambition. As far as the reformers were concerned, the day on which an old girl produced her marriage certificate, in order that she might claim an offered reward of ten shillings, was certainly an occasion for much rejoicing and ample evidence of their job well done.

Those who resisted the system or failed to conform returned to the tide of human jetsam which spilled out into the maze of narrow streets, like the garbage discharged from the tall ships into the River Mersey.

The birth of the Liverpool Juvenile Reformatory Association, soon to prove itself one of the most go-ahead in the country, had gone smoothly. It was agreed that the Earl of Derby, the Earl of Ellesmere, the Earl of Harrowby and Lord Ravenscroft be invited to become patrons. The men in attendance bowed their heads in prayer to thank the Almighty for his guidance, and respectfully to solicit His continued help. By the light of the gas lamps their pocket watches revealed the lateness of the hour. They had talked far longer than they had intended.

TRAINING SHIP

Making Ready the Akbar

It was the end of the glory days. Around the middle of the nineteenth century the Admiralty found itself with an embarrassing surfeit of its sturdy old wooden-wall vessels. Yet a new role for them was emerging from earnest discussions on dry land, a role that would require patience not courage, that would put children not men below decks, an extraordinary move that would surprise the nation with its ingenious novelty.

The ships which helped to rule the waves would now help to rule awkward and recalcitrant children. They would be turned into floating reformatories. By 1874 there were seven such reformatory ships, on loan from the Admiralty, in service in British ports and harbours. The severity of a naval type of control and training had its appeal, but the main advantage over a land reformatory was the stretch of water which separated young criminals from their former association with evil influences, and placed them in a confined space under the immediate authority of those determined to reform by discipline, strict habits of industry, religious studies, virtue, honesty and training in self control and manly independence.

The Akbar was the first to arrive on the Mersey scene, mainly due to the efforts of Mr John Clint, a local ship owner. Originally a teak-built Indiaman, constructed in Bombay in 1801, the ship had been bought by the Royal Navy for service as a 38-gun frigate under the name of Cornwallis and had served in various expeditions against the Dutch East Indies. In 1811 a new Cornwallis with almost twice the number of guns was launched and the old ship was renamed Akbar. During the war with America in 1812 her role became that of a troopship, riding the heaving Atlantic with cargoes of militia reinforcements and munitions packed together in conditions of frightful discomfort and unbelievable misery. A quieter period followed as a lazaretto (quarantine ship) in harbour service in Milford Haven.

Between 1834 and 1855 the Akbar was on quarantine service at Liverpool. With visiting ships from all over the world, the possibility of an outbreak of bubonic plague was an ever-present headache for the local authorities. As it was, periodic explosions of cholera, typhus and the dreaded smallpox with its resultant disfigurement were a frightening reality. Smallpox was a nationwide problem in the nineteenth century: in January 1871 900 smallpox cases in London alone were reported to the Poor Law Board, and a newspaper of 1855 advertised: "Smallpox Marks: These unfortunate disfigurements entirely removed from the face after a few applications in the Indian Cream prepared by the late Dr Phillip and sold by his orphan daughter Emma." Optimists could send off five shillings in stamps to Emma at an address in Lambeth. The authorities, more realistically, tried to combat the problem at source, with at least ten quarantine hulks moored off Rock Ferry at various times between 1824 and 1863 - at one stage there were six employed simultaneously.

Mr Clint and his four Committee members inspected the Akbar on a mellow July day in 1855, and they were appalled by her condition. The upper deck, which was completely rotten, would have to be removed and there was much work to be done before they could even begin to mast and spar her. That they were willing to tackle such a formidable task at all says much for their strength of purpose and faith that the good Lord would support them. It was planned to receive initially 100 boys aged between 12 and 15 years, and the estimated cost of making the grim old ship habitable and secure was £1,003 19s 4d, a figure which finally topped £2,000. As it was, the Akbar served her new purpose for only six years before the crumbling timbers became a safety hazard and she was towed away to a local breaker's yard, to be replaced by Akbar the Second.

By 15th November, 1855, the first Akbar was in a condition to receive staff. They had to be "persons of sober life and conversation, and free from drunkenness, profane cursing and swearing, lewdness and other dissolute immoral or disorderly practices." Mr Edward Hambleton was appointed superintendent at a salary of £80 a year, it being understood that his wife and child might live on board and be supplied with rations in no wise different from those of the boys. He was to be assisted by a schoolmaster to be paid £50 a year with board and lodgings, a boatswain, joiner, cook and two seamen, with additional help to be hired as the number of boys on board increased. Mr Trevor Roper was appointed honorary surgeon, a job that was to prove most onerous and, after 12 months gratuitous service, he was paid at the rate of 3/6d a head, without medicine, on the average number of persons on board throughout the year.

With typical Victorian imperiousness, the Committee decided that the superintendent would have a best suit to be worn on Sundays, Christmas Day and Good Friday and on such occasions as the Committee might from time to time direct. This comprised one blue frock coat with gilt buttons, like those worn by captains of mail steamers, one blue waistcoat with smaller gilt buttons, a pair of blue trousers and a cap with a gold band and an oil-skin cover for wet weather. On less auspicious occasions he would wear a blue frock coat without gilt buttons, blue trousers and a cap with a gold band. He must never be seen on board without his coat.

The boatswain and petty officers were allowed two suits consisting of one round blue jacket with gilt buttons, one blue waistcoat and trousers and a cap with a gilt band, narrower than the superintendent's, and an oil skin cover. One of these suits must be kept for best and must be worn only when the superintendent was wearing his best suit.

When the officers preferred, they could substitute a white waistcoat and gilt buttons and white trousers in place of the blue, the waistcoats being made with eyelet holes to facilitate the button change. The Committee covered the cost of one suit only. After 6 months, if the officer was still in their employ, the suit would become his own property. However, it had to be worn for a further twelve months before a second "best suit" was provided and the old one then used for daily wear.

The schoolmaster was supplied with a black coat and ordered that he must dress at all times in plain and subdued clothes.

The boys had to wear blue trousers and guernseys and caps for every day, the caps to be replaced by glazed hats when they manned the boats, attended church or assembled on deck for the inspection of official visitors or members of the Committee. Each lad was to have one change of linen.

The ship was officially ready for business on 8th January, 1856, with the arrival of the requisite certificate from the Home Secretary, certifying the school frigate "Akbar" as a reformatory within the meaning of the Youthful Offenders Act 17 & 18 Vic.86.

Paying the Price

That there was a need for such an establishment was soon apparent from the number of inquiries as to conditions of entry from all over the country. They came from many quarters: magistrates wishing to know whether the Committee would receive boys sentenced by them; police seeking secure accommodation for runaway boys housed temporarily in workhouses; other reformatories needing harsher discipline and control for the irrepressible; pleas for help from the guardians of destitute children, and parents who could no longer cope with offspring out of control.

A letter from a man aged 65 begged the Committee to take his 12 year old son Horatio. "He will not remain at home and, when he does make his appearance, he is quite unruly and unmanageable and pilfers whatever he can lay his hands on. I have only a pension of 3/6d a week to live on and therefore I am unable to pay anything." With the current price of cheese at 6d a pound, bacon 5d a pound, bread 5d for a 4 pound loaf, butter 8d a pound and cod and sprats at 2d a pound, to exist at all must have been enough of a problem to handle, without the misbehaviour of Horatio, who was one of the first twenty boys admitted on board. A London surgeon pleaded for the admission of his over-indulged rascally son of 13 years, in order to improve his ways. Another early arrival was Samuel aged 10, younger than the Committee wished to have on board, but the special circumstances of the case were something of a challenge to the reformers. Samuel's father wrote that he was quite unable to control his son's vicious propensities and his offer to pay 3/6d per week for the boy's maintenance was accepted.

Parents were expected to contribute, according to their means, up to 5/- a week. In cases of failure to pay, the courts had the power to make an order for payment, withhold goods, or commit the offenders to prison if necessary. The State made a grant to schools inspected and certified by one of Her Majesty's Inspectors of Prisons, which worked out in the region of 5/- a head for boys.

Financial contributions by local authorities both to the establishment of reformatories and to the upkeep of children in them began in 1857. Eleven years later, the average cost per head for the upkeep of 180 boys on board worked out at 7/6d per week. The schools relied greatly on public donations and subscriptions

The Akbar, a wooden lockup anchored a third of a mile offshore. Home and, it was hoped, reformation for 300 recalcitrant boys. Photographed from the shore at Rock Ferry

to cover costs and every effort was made by the Committee to cajole and beg money from their friends and from the moneyed residents of Liverpool. The response was never very impressive, for not everyone was so fired with philanthropic enthusiasm. The most generous were happy to send along turnips, windfall apples, rhubarb and their abundance of garden vegetables which proved manna from heaven to a ship of hungry lads, ticking along on a basic diet of small portions of ship's biscuits, suet pudding, gruel, cocoa and bullock's head meat. Enthused the captain at one annual meeting: "Many thanks to friends for various presents including fruit and vegetables. I would like to remind friends who have gardens, that, much which they throw away, if sent to the Akbar would be gratefully received by me and equally gratefully consumed by the boys."

Like a thrifty housewife with a large family to feed, the Committee considered every penny-scrimping idea in an effort to prune down expenditure: "January 11th 1858 - Try beef at 5½d a pound: April 1862 - Cook to undertake the barber's work which will save 15/- per month: 1863 - Committee understands that new boots can be bought cheap for cash at 5/6d and appear as good as those for which we have paid 7/-, 8/- and 9/-. Try them. Understand potatoes can be bought for 1/10d a bushel equal to those for which Hall and Son are paid 4/3d - change supplier." "July 1864 - Occasional washing of night shirts on shore approved but additional new ones objected to." Practical gifts for ship improvements to keep down costs were gratefully received. There was a yearly present of three bolts of canvas, casks of paint, oil and varnish. In 1858, a committee member presented the ship with a suit of top gallant sails and in the same year, the Storekeeper General of the Navy despatched two harbour cutters for the Akbar's use.

The chairman was always calling attention to the continued falling off in the subscription list and venturing to hope that more assistance in this way would be forthcoming in the ensuing year. By 1882 three schools within the Liverpool Reformatory Association had been established, and out of an expenditure of £8,000 subscriptions from the citizens of Liverpool themselves totalled less than £250. Four years later, at the 31st annual meeting, the Mayor remarked on the continued decline of subscriptions to the Association, and appealed for monies, stressing, "It would be a pity if the good work of the Association should be crippled by lack of funds."

In the early years, reformatories were to some extent on trial, and there were not a few persons who believed that such establishments were a mistake. This was referred to by Mr Samuel Martin at the annual general meeting of the Association in 1865. "I am sorry to see lately a spirit abroad rather depreciating reformatories. People have said to me, 'Is it true you are doing some good? But you are not doing the amount of good you ought to effect, considering the labour and money expended upon these institutions!' I told them of the scores of hundreds of boys and girls that have been taken from their haunts of vice and after passing time in reformatories are earning their living and likely to become useful members of society. The opponents then say, 'Look at the mass of crime and vice that still exists,' but they did not take into consideration the increase in the population." He trusted that the time would never come when the committees of reformatories were so pauperised that they would relax their efforts, much less that the time should come when they would fold their arms and say that it was impossible for them to deal with an evil of such magnitude.

Attempts at Escape

To be eligible for admission to floating reformatories the lads had to be as strong and able-bodied as their deprived status in society would allow, and as a consequence they were on the whole more tough, rough and adventurous than their land reformatory counterparts.

Some, of course, went there determined to escape. To do so from the Akbar, moored off Rock Ferry on the Cheshire side of the Mersey, meant a third of a mile swim in murky waters with the added challenge of dangerous tides, or a row to freedom in a small boat, lowered at great risk during the hours of darkness in the hope of avoiding the eagle eye of the ship's officer. If caught, punishment was severe: a three day diet of bread and water in solitary confinement in the ship's cell, plus a flogging, or 12 cuts with a birch rod, at times increased to 18 with the Committee's special permission. It was not unusual for lads to be brought before the magistrates and committed to gaol for the offence of "running". Absconding or unruly conduct could be punished by a prison sentence of up to three months.

With a bounty of 20/- a head on all runaways, and instructions from the Reformatory Committee to detain any boy without a pass stating the duty to which he had been entrusted, the police were extra vigilant. The occasional boy who managed to reach home was usually given an unsympathetic thrashing by his father and promptly returned on board. Any more compassionate parent paying heed to a runaway's plea for help was brought before the magistrate and sentenced to pay a substantial amount of money, or go to gaol for a month for harbouring him.

Yet the magnetism of the watery escape route invited contest throughout the history of the Akbar. Several lads drowned in their bid for freedom. Others were swept out to sea in tossing boats, after capricious winds snatched away the oars from frozen fingers. Their clothing and poor physique were no match for the elements, and even the more fortunate who were plucked from the waves by a passing ship, or foundered on distant banks, were overcome with sickness and exposure.

Every exploit was duly reported to the Committee: "August 26th 1889 - Fishwick and Thorn absconded over the side on the 12th.

Their descriptions were at once sent to the police and a reward offered. Fishwick was arrested in Liverpool, the same afternoon. He had swum ashore and concealed himself in a fishing boat for two hours. Half-way to shore Thorn became distressed and Fishwick gave him a cork lifebelt that he had on but, whilst Thorn was pulling it on, down he went and never rose again. His body was found floating in the river and an inquest recorded the verdict 'accidentally drowned'. Fishwick was punished with 18 cuts of the cane and one day in cells. He is far from being a bad lad, he has a vile temper which he is sometimes unable to control, but I feel pretty confident however that we will make a good man of him."

"Thorn was always giving trouble in small matters and was dirty, careless and lazy, he was sent to Akbar 21 months since for attempting to set fire to an industrial school in Manchester, where he was confined."

It was hardly an epitaph to stir the reformers into a state of mourning. On that track record, Thorn would have seemed destined to join the 25% who failed the system.

The sheer ingenuity of the boys proved a constant challenge to those in authority. Two lads, handcuffed and confined to the cell, managed, with the expertise of Houdini, to slip the heavy iron cuffs, remove the bars from a minute window and wriggle out to freedom. Their liberty was short-lived and the captain's report of November 3rd 1862 noted: "For attempting to abscond Stephens and Smith had each a dozen with the 'Cat'." In all probability, on the next spell of detention in the cell, they would be in leg irons as well.

In spite of increased punishment to subdue their spirit, the more adventurous continued to abscond. One lad, William, a persistent escapee, became so expert a swimmer that during the latter years of his detention, he won acclaim and a medal for the Akbar in swimming contests with other reformatory schools. There were, however, occasions when a runaway, after existing on gutter scraps for a few days, decided that the spartan comforts and diet of the Akbar were preferable to the harsh reality of the world outside, and returned voluntarily to plead forgiveness and accept his deserts.

Pastimes and Perils

The problem of boredom was immense. How does one keep busy 300 boys bursting with energy from five in the morning until eight o'clock bedtime, in a wooden prison anchored a third of a mile offshore? Finding them things to do was a constant challenge for those in control.

Decks were scrubbed repeatedly with stone, and later with coconut husks, the latter proving less wearing on the deck surfaces. The boys made and repaired their own clothing. In 1858 they made 976 pieces of clothing, 180 pairs of new shoes and repaired 276 pairs. They also made 18 sea-chests. To provide winter employment in 1856, a supply of junk was obtained for conversion into oakum. The boys were paid 1/- a hundred-weight. The money was divided between them, and the same amount shared among the men. Teasing and splitting the old rope was a filthy job, shredding the skin off frozen fingers, and happily it was abandoned in 1862, after the captain reported: "The Oakum is not all sold. It injures the boys' clothing and makes them very dirty." Instead, tailoring orders were accepted from the prestigious Conway, a vessel which frequently provided additional work opportunities. For example, in 1863 thirty Akbar lads were loaned to that ship to help clean up before the return of the elite pupils, cadets in training for the Royal Navy and Merchant Service.

In the hold, illuminated by oil lamps on winter evenings, the boys played draughts or bagatelle and read such magazines as the "British Workman", the "Band of Hope Review", the "Illustrated News" and "Animals Friend", two copies of which were donated monthly by the Birkenhead branch of the Prevention of Cruelty to Animals. On Sunday their attention was directed to bible study, text books with religious messages, and other volumes extolling the virtues of being kind, honest, hard working and leading clean and godly lives. The boys were allowed access

Akbar boys - smartly attired in their best "on parade" outfits

to a gift of 200 volumes of "amusing" books, donated in 1860 by the free lending library, only after the Committee had vetted each copy for any hint of salacity.

Other recreational activities consisted of spelling bees, magic lantern shows, and lectures on such subjects as "Temperance and the Evils of Drink", "Self Made Men", "Missionary Work in India", and "Honesty is the Best Policy". Two of the boys received prizes from Miss Weston, known as the "Sailor's Friend", for most creditable essays on Temperance subjects! Gentlemen visitors recited and sang suitable songs of that era and a rapturous ovation from delighted boys was reported in every case, irrespective of the quality of the performance. One of the most popular speakers was a Captain Stephens, who not only described life on board his ship but also gave the boys a treat of "plum duff and pears"!

A sing-song to the accompaniment of the harmonium was greatly enjoyed. The boys sang heartily and their voices frequently overwhelmed the accompaniment. In March 1858, when there were 145 boys on board, it was agreed that the old harmonium should be replaced with a new one as it was "no longer powerful enough for the voices of so many boys".

In June 1858, Captain Fenwick was authorised to purchase such musical instruments as might be necessary for a band, the amount not to exceed six pounds, and to hire a bandmaster. A full brass band developed and its excellence made it a popular attraction at local church bazaars and other functions. A request by the managers of the Rock Ferry Steamers for its use on Good Friday was curtly refused with a note to say that that day should be devoted to Holy Observance! In September 1874, the Band was invited to Leasowe Castle to play before HRH the Duke of Edinburgh. It was a most important day in the history of the band and both staff and boys were delighted when the Duke expressed himself highly pleased with their performance. By 1881, the pounding on the drum had taken its toll and permission was given to buy a replacement. The brass band continued for another 29 years, when it was replaced by a Bugle Corps.

Winter or summer, once a week was bath night in the fresh cold water in wooden tanks. There were many occasions when the ice was hacked away to allow the boys the privilege of their dip, but on hot steamy days, when the millpond surface of the surrounding water reflected the heat haze, the most popular pastime was swimming.

In 1874, permission was given for the boys to use the Indefatigable's floating bath for an annual fee of £20. Every effort was made to teach each boy to swim and in 1876, of the 190 boys on board, 134 had learned. The boys were regular recipients of medals donated by the Liverpool Humane Society, for bravely jumping into the Mersey and rescuing comrades who, being non-swimmers, were in danger of drowning. Nevertheless, over the years, a considerable number of boys perished below the

Mersey waves. One such happening was reported thus: "A gloom was cast over the ship in July by the accidental drowning of two boys while bathing with others from the beach at New Ferry. One had ventured out rather far, and appeared in difficulties when his friend went to help him, but before a boat could reach them they had both disappeared. Their bodies were recovered some days after. The boys and others have placed a neat tablet in St Peter's Church, Rock Ferry, to the memory of their two unfortunate shipmates."

There were also horrendous accidents described in the old Minute Books: "Thomas while employed in blacking a portion of the rigging was accidentally jerked off and thrown down from a height of 16 feet on to the deck, dying three hours later... Alfred fell from the main top deck and received concussion and partial jaw fracture, was recovering...Henry lost his finger by carelessly placing his hand between a boat and the ship... Benjamin fell from the main top, died same day...William, while manning the working boat, slipped and was crushed between the boat and the ship side. His body was washed up on shore... Ebenezer fell from the main top - a height of 60 feet and was taken to hospital where he has progressed favourably." A hook and ring appliance at a cost of £2 10s was ordered for Smith, who lost his arm in an Akbar accident in 1880.

The Mersey presented a ready-made opportunity for pleasurable

Each floating reformatory developed a full brass band which was much in demand for local church bazaars and other functions. The Clarence Band

pursuits. When the weather was fine the boys were allowed to use the boats after supper either for rowing or racing. In 1892 at the New Brighton Regatta, the Akbar boys won a race against the boys of the Catholic Reformatory Ship Clarence, and received as their prize a cup and money.

There were hazards, too, in living so near to the river. The tempting mussels near the Rock Ferry slip in 1892 caused five cases of enteric fever and one death from typhoid.

In 1888, following the Government Inspector's threat that no Reformatory Ship without a good playing field ashore should be allowed to hold a certificate, a field was rented at a cost of £5 a year for the purpose of football and cricket. Captain Hicks reported: "At first the majority of the lads were quite ignorant of games and preferred to do nothing, for which they evince much talent. It has involved much trouble to interest them in out-door games but the effort is fully repaid by the results shown in their every day work. As they avail themselves more constantly of the opportunities for exercise on shore, the moral tone of the boys is better now than for some years. We have played several football matches this winter, with fairly good success for sailors!"

They were so successful that in 1908 at Macclesfield sports the boys won seven silver medals and one gold medal, but there were disadvantages. On one fine Saturday evening three boys ran off from a cricket game and were not recovered until a month later, one lad travelling as far away as Exeter!

Special Treats

Some of the Akbar treats were centred on the nearby resort of New Brighton, which in those days offered all the entertainment of Blackpool but on a smaller scale. One such occasion was on September 7th 1895, when 166 of the 184 boys on board were taken for a day out. This was funded by the Committee and friends, who raised fourteen guineas for the treat. The entertainment and tea at the Palace cost £5 3s 3d, a visit to the Pavilion - 10/-; donkey and pony rides - £1; sweets - 5/-; prizes for the races, long-jump, wheelbarrow, hurdle and sack and a tug-of-war - 11/10d; pier charge at New Brighton - 10/-; and a fee to the captain of the tug "Despatch" for conveying the boys from the Akbar - 10/-. 2/- was set aside to give a special tea to the boys left behind on board ship. The balance remaining after this fun day was used for the purchase of football, cricket and gymnasium gear.

National holidays were acknowledged with special delight. For example, on the occasion of the Prince of Wales' wedding on March 10th 1863, each boy was given plum pudding and two oranges, and on July 6th 1893 there was a dinner of beef and plum pudding to celebrate the marriage of HRH the Duke of York. In 1911, the whole school joined in the Coronation procession through the town in the morning and in the sporting events which followed. Reported the captain: "The boys were allowed to mix freely with the public and when the bugle sounded at 7.15pm every boy was promptly in his place. The conduct throughout the day was exemplary."

For the good boys there were rare trips to see the new comic pantomimes, "Sinbad the Sailor", "All that Glitters is not Gold" and "Pizarro and Blackeyed Susan". Seats in the gallery cost 6d, the pit 1/- and boxes were priced at 2/-. There were special reduced prices for the parties of Akbar lads. Seventy boys were permitted to watch the Regatta at New Brighton, a spectacular affair which attracted an armada of small craft and while the crowd clapped and cheered, the Akbar band played a suitable selection of patriotic music.

Playing marbles on the upper deck was another privilege allowed for good behaviour. It was a popular pastime but indirectly caused the death of young George who, in the process of a game, was wounded by a rifle bullet fired from a boat on the river and died later on board. The matter was reported to the police and at an inquest held on the Akbar the jury brought a manslaughter charge against James Barber of the Liverpool Rowing Club, who had been using a rifle loaded with ball cartridge. The grand jury, considering the verdict of the coroner later, dismissed the charge of manslaugher.

There were many examples of special kindnesses towards the boys from outsiders. In 1889, Miss Fanny Joseph treated the boys to the pantomime at the Prince of Wales theatre and gave to each of them an orange. Mr Montague Roby invited a party of boys to the "Midget Minstrels" and the Reverend Mr Hankins, who had assisted with their religious instruction, sent a wedding card with the hope that the Committee would not object to his giving the boys a treat of plum pudding in honour of the occasion of his marriage. Friends contributed ninepence a head in 1888 for the boys to visit the Pleasure Gardens at Eastham, where there was a zoo with tigers and bears and a view of Blondin, the famous tightrope walker who had crossed the Niagara Falls.

These donations were acknowledged in 1894, in the Captain's report: "Heartiest thanks to the many friends who have helped us in various ways, some by assisting at our Winter entertainment, others by contributing money towards treats, the kind ladies who have worked articles of clothing, and to all, who have given their interest and sympathy. Their reward must surely be in the knowledge that they have shown kindness where kindness is wanted, and are helping children who, during their short lives, have had more than their share of hard knocks."

Several times a year all the good lads were invited to tea at the magnificent home of Committee member Mr John Cropper at West Dingle. The Cropper family were l aders in philanthropic activity in Liverpool: John's father, James, was a pioneer in the movement to effect the extinction of slavery in the British Dominions. John Cropper himself was one of the promoters of the scheme for starting the Akbar, and remained closely associated with its management all of his life. He lived in a mansion set in twelve acres of landscaped gardens with rolling lawns, trees, shrubs and colourful flower beds and on these special occasions the boys were allowed to wander freely, exploring the grounds and taking in with wide-eyed admiration the fine views of the ships sailing down the Mersey. They enjoyed teas of bread and butter, home-made preserves, scones and cakes, and were served by the maids of the household.

Christmas was a spell of great excitement, with everyone intent on giving the boys a good time. On December 22nd 1873, a Mr Pearson sent on board £5 with the instruction "Get what is wanted to make the boys happy." Some of the money was spent on a slice of bread for each boy! School was suspended for a fortnight and during the holidays the boys were kept occupied decorating the ship and their messes with gifts of evergreens, and twisting coloured paper into festive streamers. A large number, in charge of an officer, went ashore to play football and to slide on frozen ponds. Others, in smaller parties, visited the Liverpool Museum and were taken for strolls to gaze into shop windows filled with a fine array of Yuletide fare. Every effort was made to provide an extra special Christmas dinner, which usually consisted of a small ration of roast beef and plum

The happiest day of the year - the Akbar boys, led by their band, march smartly to their camp!

pudding. A taste of goose was a luxury introduced latterly. For every boy going to sea there was a gift of a "Housewife", a needle and thread repair kit. Other presents included religious books and illuminated cards, and socks, mufflers and mitts were donated by kindly ladies with a fondness for knitting; the South Lancashire branch of "Our Needlework Guild" sent a quantity of socks and mufflers at Christmas 1886. By 1904, every boy was having two dips into a well filled bran pie, and general gifts included a bagatelle and billiard tables, three pairs of boxing gloves, footballs, a mandoline, cakes, crackers and three large geese!

Even in the early days when there were no presents for distribution, each child received an orange and apple on Christmas morning, and as time advanced gifts for the Akbar became more plentiful. The boys enjoyed luxuries such as boxes of currants and raisins, a 140-pound bag of nuts, barrels of apples, 56 pounds of sweets, boxes of oranges and dates, bags of figs and an abundance of plum puddings and boxes of crackers.

Special prizes were introduced to encourage commendable behaviour. Writing desks were awarded for Good Conduct and Athletics, and one was kept specially for the tidiest boy on the ship. Two bibles were given to the boys who were most proficient in Religious Knowledge. The most coveted prize of all was a handsome silver watch and chain donated yearly for "Good and Manly Conduct". It was noted by the captain, in 1891, that several recipients of this award had been on board, all of whom were proudly wearing their watches!

The only women on board were the female members of the captain's family who lived a purdah-like existence in special but uncomfortable quarters situated well away from the boys. Some of the wives were more kindly than others, mixing with the lads and on occasions doling out treats. Daughters were forbidden to speak to the boys, if indeed they ever had the opportunity!

The Hicks family were different. Mrs Hicks was a warm, kindly woman and the boys adored her. The event of the year in 1898 was when she opened a tuck shop on board. It was entirely her own work and such a huge success that the HM Inspector commented: "A lad can buy any article from a red herring to a pocket handkerchief for a copper. As these coppers are not very numerous, the lads appreciate being able to buy their sweets, ginger beer and treats, in many cases at less than wholesale price. It has brought Mrs Hicks into closer contact with boys, as much talking can be done over the sale of an ounce of toffee. It enables the lads to better show their kindly feeling one to another and brings out the better side of their humanity." Her daughter inherited much of her benignity and, with the help of friends, frequently organised theatrical performances in Rock Ferry to raise money for extra treats for the lads. The magnificent sum of £15 enabled the boys to have their own magic lantern at Christmas 1898.

Captain Hicks, in common with so many of the staff on board, fell victim to the atrocious living conditions. His constitution was no match for the sweat shop conditions of summer, the bitter damp days of winter and the ever-present infection within the wooden walls. In August 1902 he was given six months' leave in a final attempt to recuperate his failing health. This act of generosity by the Committee, who rated him highly, was to no avail, for he died within a month.

The funeral reflected the Captain's worthy character and the esteem in which he was held. A large number of the boys attended, with the Bugle Corps playing a solemn lament and the Honorable Captain Stanhope of HMS Eaglet sending along a firing party. Mrs Hicks was given a cheque for £112 10s in appreciation of her husband's services. Many of the boys wept broken-heartedly when Mrs Hicks and her family finally packed their bags and clambered down into the boat to be taken ashore.

The new commander of the Akbar was Captain G L Bennett, who took over on November 14th 1902 at a salary of £300 per annum with £42 6s for rations.

Famous Visitors

Because the Akbar was so closely moored to the more influential Conway, it was ideally placed to cream off many of the latter's illustrious visitors. There were visits from the Prince of Wales, the Sultan of Zanzibar, the Duke of Edinburgh and in 1861, Prince Albert was escorted on board under the guidance of the Mayor and expressed his "approbation of the purpose of the Institution," praised the order and cleanliness of all on board, and promised the boys buns and apples. Other honoured guests included the Lords of the Admiralty, the Bishop of Sydney, the Japanese Ambassador, the Earl of Devon, Lords Carnarvon, Derby and Clarendon, the Marquis of Westminster and an American gentleman, the Honorable Mr Pearse, calling on an order from the Secretary of State to see the ship.

Nearly all the visitors had their own message of inspiration. Rear Admiral Dacres GB, before leaving addressed these few words of encouragement to the boys: "I have always impressed among my sons and those whom I have instructed the importance of truth and honesty, without which it is impossible for anyone to succeed in life. I have had the command of thousands of men, and never found any difficulty with a man who is truthful and honest. People might laugh at so much importance being attached to truth and honesty, but they can depend upon it, otherwise they come to grief as you Reformatory boys have found out. However, boys on board the Akbar should thank God you have been sent to such an Institution, where you receive instruction the like of which you have never before enjoyed, and this will give you the opportunity of being fairly launched in life."

The visit of the Duke of Edinburgh on 23rd June 1896 received wide press coverage and brought with it a special tribute for the

Akbar. In particular, the abstemious conduct of four of its lads won Royal approval for resisting the temptation to join in the city-wide tipple in honour of the Royal visitor! The press reported:

"It was ten minutes of 12 o'clock when the Duke of Edinburgh re-embarked on board the Alert at Birkenhead Ferry, after leaving the ship building yard of Messrs Laird Bros. At this time the atmosphere was remarkably clear, and a brilliant sunshine imparted great beauty to the scene on the river. Before quitting the Mersey his Royal Highness had determined to pay a visit to the Akbar and Clarence, the Reformatory ships and the training ship Indefatigable; the Alert steamed up the river, and in passing her Majesty's ship Donegal, a royal salute was fired from the vessel, the band having previously played 'God Save the Queen'. Reaching first the Akbar, the Prince proceeded on board and was received by Captain Borland RN the Master, and members of the Committee.

On board the Akbar there were 186 boys, the whole of whom had an exceedingly clean and smart appearance. The Prince having made a hurried inspection of the ship, Mr S R Graves, MP for Wavertree, read to his Royal Highness the following letter:- 'To

Famous visitors were honoured with the display of a large number of the boys, clean and smart of appearance, manning the yards on the Clarence

S R Graves Esq, MP. Wavertree Board of Health Public Offices, June 23, 1866. Sir - In returning the four boys to the Akbar yesterday, I understand the Prince was due to visit them today and as they were under my care while here, I beg to mention that they were under great temptation, as several parties wished to give them drink, but in all cases they refused to take anything, according to my instructions. The names of the boys are John Bell, Petty Officer; John Fairbrother, John Davies and Arthur Luckman. If you would be kind enough to recommend them to the Captain you would oblige your humble servant, Andrew Young.'

His Royal Highness replied; 'Captain Borland, it gives me much pleasure to hear such a satisfactory report of the conduct of these four boys whilst on shore. It reflects great credit on the boys themselves, and I hope that their example will be emulated by their companions on board.'

Upon his Royal Highness leaving the Akbar, the greater number of the boys manned the yards, whilst another party of them sang 'God Save the Queen' in beautiful style."

Some of the visitors left donations for special treats. On September 16th 1872, Sir George and Lady Barrow visited and "seemed much pleased". Lady Barrow addressed the 173 boys and proffered £1 for the Library fund, and Sir George handed over £1 to give the boys a meal of bread! He expressed his surprise at seeing the boys looking so well, stating that such erroneous ideas that the ship was a prison and not a school should at once be dispelled.

An Exclusive Training

Each boy attended class for not less than three hours a day to learn reading, spelling and cyphering. The sole teacher, in the early days, had a formidable task. This was illustrated in 1858, when the then schoolmaster was noted as being "inadequate to control and educate so large a number of boys as there are now on board," and so he was replaced by a "younger and more active" man. At that time there were 141 boys in class. The majority of these were illiterate, and one could sense a hint of sympathy for the unfortunate schoolmaster in the Committee's decision to reward him with a gratuity of £2 for two years of "faithful" service.

All the boys received instruction in Practical Seamanship. In 1866, when the Rock Ferry boatmen went on strike for more wages, an application to the captain for Akbar lads to work the steamers was readily agreed and two boys were sent to each boat, resulting in the receipt of a most satisfactory letter regarding their conduct and £6 3s 2d for their hire.

A naval officer, appointed in 1894 by the Admiralty to inspect the ship in Nautical Exercises, expressed himself "surprised and satisfied with all I have seen."

In the early days the lads were trained for the Merchant Service. The Navy, on the whole, refused to accept Reformatory lads, considering them not good enough, although a number did find their way into the Navy as stokers. However, some were admitted after they had proved their worth at sea by producing a "good" discharge certificate.

The seamanship instruction on board was of a particularly high standard and included learning the points of the compass; knotting and splicing with practice on wire rope; tuition in the use of the palm and needle; canvas stitching and hammock making; and there was plenty of experience in summer of sail drill aloft. Heaving the lead was carried out from one of the ship's boats and during the year 1896 the boys fitted a new mizen top-mast. In that winter the normal distribution of a watch at nautical instruction was as follows: sailmakers, 10; compass class, 5; monkey topsail, 5; knotting and splicing, 23; tailors, 13; carpenters, 2; cooks, 4; duty boys and boat crews making up the remainder. A class of signal instruction was added in 1905, and the ship was presented with a set of Commercial Code Flags and the Code Signal.

In 1898, out of 395 old hands heard of during that year, one was a captain, one a master's mate in the American Navy and two quartermasters in American Revenue Cruisers. One was a chief mate and there were three first mates, four second mates, three third mates, two boatswains, one sailmaker, seventy-one able seamen, seventy-six ordinary seamen, three firemen, three stewards, one quartermaster, one leading stoker RN, seven stokers RN, one able seaman RN, one boy RN, two Army sergeants, two lance-corporals, eight Army privates, two bandsmen, one policeman, two engine-drivers, one collier, two apprentices (sea), two letter carriers, one contractor, two railway porters, one cook, four painters and decorators, one fish hawker, one hundred and fourteen labourers, two shoe blacks, four carters, one stone cutter, one greaser and fifty-five tradesmen. One boy, discharged thirty-two years earlier, was a prosperous builder paying more than £90 a week in wages; another boy finished up a general in the Chinese Army!

A cookery class was started in 1908 to assist the Akbar boys in their training as cooks and stewards, and the Officers' Mess was allowed £1 a month for eating the food dished up by the class!

After a year's detention, boys of exemplary behaviour were granted leave. In 1857, 31 country boys were allowed home leave for between 10 and 14 days. Of 126 Liverpool boys due for turns of one-day leave, two of them had this privilege withdrawn because of unsatisfactory conduct, and one boy had to forfeit his leave because it was undesirable that he should visit home, owing to the bad character of his friends. It was noted that the privilege of leave had produced a marked improvement in the health, conduct and disposition of the boys which was reflected in their "smart and cheerful" work on ship. By 1896, the boys were being sent on errands ashore to "test their moral courage and powers of self-control". In their bright uniforms with shaved heads they were closely observed and the slightest hint of bad manners or misbehaviour was reported by the public.

The Committee members were very selective as to whom they allowed on board the Akbar, whether as inmates or visitors. Some of their decisions reflected appalling bigotry which today would heap upon them all the fury of Race Relations and Civil Liberties campaigners.

In June 1856, by which time there were 50 boys in confinement, a request for the admission of a "boy of colour" was refused on the grounds that "the discipline of the ship is at present so imperfect such a boy be not received but that the committee will be glad to receive any other."

The quarterly Sunday visit of the boys' friends, with as many as 150 travelling by steamer to the ship, was a privilege under constant review by the Committee. All were carefully vetted to exclude "improper people who come on board to visit no-one in particular," and there were several instances of the favour being withdrawn. One such occasion was on August 24th 1863, a calamitous day when 8 boys out of 164 had made their escape. A furious captain stopped all visiting and claimed all reward monies to assist in defraying the expense incurred in the recapture of the runaways. Vistors were banned yet again in April 1864, for having brought vermin on board.

Former inmates of doubtful character who called were immediately removed and one notoriously bad lad, who had come on board with a friend with evil intent, was hosed out of the ship with a "water cannon". There was no room either for George, a 13-year-old petty thief who was most anxious to join his brother. Birds of a feather flocking together could cause extra trouble!

Roman Catholics were not generally welcome in the early days. The Committee reluctantly agreed to accept two Roman Catholic boys, but when the Reverend Father Brown, a Birkenhead priest, wrote to the Akbar captain asking to visit the two boys, he received a curt reply from the Secretary: "As the Act of Parliament left the religious instruction in the hands of the Committee, they respectfully declined Mr Brown's interference."

By 1863, the increase in the number of applications for the admission of Roman Catholic delinquents to Protestant Akbar was causing concern. Officials at the borough gaol requested admission of eight Roman Catholic boys for whom no other reformatory could be found, and who would have to be sent back to their parents "in all probability to evil courses". The request was refused, and the superintendents of all three reformatory schools within the Association were instructed not to receive any more Roman Catholics, until the Committee had taken legal advice as to the responsibility of the Association regarding compulsory visits of Ministers of Religion under the Reformatory Act.

It was the opinion of the Liverpool Recorder that any claim by a Roman Catholic priest to be admitted on board the Akbar with a view to the religious teaching of Roman Catholic boys was out of order. This was confirmed by legal counsel. The Association at that time received no grant under the Reformatory Act regulations, preferring to accept a Corporation grant from surplus funds under the Municipal Act. Nor had they entered into an officially drawn-up contract with any committee of justices or borough council to receive and detain offenders; instead there was only a special agreement to accept them from time to time, in consideration of periodical payments. Thus reassured of their independence, the Committee agreed to find room for a limited number of Roman Catholic children "only because a Roman Catholic reformatory cannot be found for them," and subject to the controlling Rules of the Association. They resolved further not to enter into any contract which might bring them within the provisions of the Act. As far as the lads of the Akbar were concerned, he who led them along the path of righteousness must be strictly Church of England.

A Harsh Discipline

The accommodation problem for Roman Catholic boy delinquents was resolved in March 1864, when a number of prominent Roman Catholics on Merseyside decided to provide a reformatory ship of their own. She was the Clarence, taking up position a third of a mile off Rock Ferry, alongside the Akbar, the Indefatigable (a ship used for the training of non-delinquent orphans and boys in poor circumstances) and, somewhat incongruously, the Conway, a school frigate for training the sons of gentlemen as future officers.

The Clarence was burnt out at her moorings in January 1884, a not uncommon ending for a reformatory ship and one of the hazards of occupation by a large number of restless and undisciplined boys. Her successor, provided in 1884, suffered a similar fate. In July 1899, she too went up in flames and was sunk by gunfire at noon on the following day. It was a spectacular display and greatly enjoyed by those Akbar boys who were able to watch. As a consequence, fire precautions and discipline on board the Akbar were tightened.

There were several attempts to fire the Akbar, but the flames were doused before they took much of a hold. One such incident was on August 24th 1877, when there were 189 boys on board. The captain reported: "A little after 6am I was awoke by an alarm of fire and immediately slipped on a dressing gown and ran down to the seat of the fire which was in the after hold and in three distinct places. The fire was made up on a lot of odds and ends of rope which we call shakings and which were saturated with tar.

"Mr Webb and Mr Allen were most energetic at the seat of the fire, the latter being almost exhausted and smothered with smoke.

Fortunately having fire quarters and stations every night we had the evening before filled wash deck tubs with water, so that being very prompt we had got the fire well under before we got the hoses from the pumps and I think it must have been discovered almost immediately it was lighted. This, of course, was after the boys were up in the morning, they behaved well and there was no sort of panic, but had it happened in the night things might have had a very different result." The lad responsible was sentenced at Chester Assizes to 18 months imprisonment with hard labour.

With sixty tons of coal on board for cooking and heating purposes and casks of oil to fuel the lamps which had replaced the old-style candles in lantern holders, fire was always a possibility. In 1875, after an upturned oil lamp caused the loss by fire of a training ship in the Thames, the Akbar acquired leather hoses and a portable fire engine. Ten years later the ship received a gift of twelve fire extinguishing hand grenades. A lighted lamp ignited the curtains in the senior instructor's cabin in 1903 and the fire spread rapidly to the upper part of the portside of the main deck. It was just as well that a few months earlier the Committee had accepted an offer from the Birkenhead Corporation Fire Brigade to help extinguish any Akbar fires, on the understanding that the Salvage Association would convey their men and appliances to the scene, and that all expenses would be covered.

On board the Akbar rascally behaviour was combatted with a severity of punishment which showed little compassion for the

Training ship Wellesley on fire in the Tyne in March 1914. The Wellesley, formerly HMS Boscawen, had been used for training boys for the Mercantile Marine since 1873

youth of the offender. A 14-year-old Akbar lad, guilty of repeated thefts from the storeroom and cabins, was in 1859 tried at the Sessions and sentenced to seven years penal servitude! Eleven years later, a 13-year-old who broke into the store and stole onions was immediately sent to the Birkenhead "lock up" and subsequently despatched to Chester Castle to serve three months hard labour. Absconders were punished with 18 months hard labour, and boys who worked ashore and spent some of their wages instead of handing them over to the captain were flogged, locked in a cell at dark every night and released at daylight.

In 1862, for attempting to abscond, George was given "a dozen with the cat." Nelson, who absconded in fear of being flogged for a tobacco offence, was retaken and given a "double flogging".

The parents of free (uncommitted) boys were warned in advance of the severe retribution meted out to those lads who did not yield to the Akbar's brand of discipline. Cautionary messages were forwarded in 1858 to two fathers, one a captain of the Isle of Man Steam Packet and the other a surgeon. They were asked to contribute 6/- a week towards maintenance and 20/- for clothing and told that the Committee must be given their authority to detain the lads, both aged 11, for twelve months.

Most of the boys were controllable. They accepted without question the class structure of the time, which established their role in a society from which they expected little. They were naturally inclined to defer to persons in authority, especially to those of a higher social class whom they met in a situation designed to emphasis their difference.

Mutiny

There were a few boys, however, who were alienated against any form of control and when trouble broke out they excelled in leadership. The submissive were easily influenced by the bully boys and there were several examples of lads being persuaded to follow the road to lawlessness.

Such was the case on September 25th 1887, when mutiny broke out on board the Akbar. Captain Symons was on leave at the time and the 143 boys on board were under the care of the Chief Officer, Mr Callender. The first hint that trouble might be in the offing came when several "evil-disposed" boys suddenly downed tools and refused to obey orders. The leaders moved swiftly throughout the ship, enticing others to join them and arm themselves with sticks, belaying pins and pieces of wood. The officers were not equal to the threat and retreated from the army of belligerent, taunting boys, who were soon able to get the upper hand. Cheering lads hacked down the door of the stores and equipped themselves with clothing before breaking into the Captain's cabin and stealing, among other articles, his wife's jewellery. Seventeen of the ringleaders lowered a boat and enjoyed several days of freedom before being recaptured.

One of the ringleaders, Mullin, charged before the Stipendiary Magistrate with having wilfully damaged some of the ship's fittings, and disobeying orders, was sentenced to three months hard labour. Another lad, charged with stealing clothing, received the same sentence and both were refused re-admittance to the Akbar.

The revolt made newspaper headlines with criticism of the reformers and controversy regarding their system of control. When ten more of the ringleaders pleaded guilty to mutinous conduct before Mr Justice Day, at Liverpool Winter Assizes, he declined to punish them further, stating that "the discipline of the Akbar is defective, the staff of officers inadequate, and the whole matter characterises a want of firmness and determination on the part of the staff which, if exhibited at the right time, might easily have quelled the whole disturbance." The Committee was shocked by the comment of the Judge, and authorised the Secretary to write to the newspapers explaining the object of their institutions.

The boys who were returned on board were severely punished. They received 18 cuts apiece and a sojourn in solitary confinement in a darkened cell situated in the bowels of the old ship, on a diet of ship's biscuit and water.

There was little consolation for the reformers in the report of HM Inspector Colonel Inglis, despatched by the Government to investigate the happening, which was rapidly developing into a nationwide scandal. He reported: "Eighteen eighty-seven has been a year of great trial for the Akbar. The good discipline which has for so many years distinguished this ship, almost entirely broke down. The cause may readily be traced to a want of firmness and energy in dealing with a mere handful of vicious and depraved youths who would have at once succumbed to a resolute and determined effort to bring them to their senses. Good order had been secured for so long on board this ship by moderate measures that it was supposed that there never could come a moment when violence and tumult would have to be met by a display of superior force physically as well as morally. Such a moment arrived, and the officers were unable to handle the occasion. The boys were in command and this ought never to have been allowed. In the absence of the captain, a mutinous spirit was shown and the officers were completely defied. The staff have now been strengthened accordingly but it will be some time before the ship recovers its ordinary tranquility, and probably not without complete re-organisation and a new commander." Captain Symons was ordered to report on the sufficiency of all his staff to enforce order and their capability for their duties. An additional officer and two night watchmen were appointed.

At the 33rd Annual Meeting of the Liverpool Reformatory Association Mr R S Blease referred to the Akbar mutiny in his Secretary's report: "It is hoped that good conduct and order will soon be restored. These cases of unruly behaviour arise from the influence and example of older lads, some very big boys for fourteen, fifteen or sixteen, who, owing to their advanced age when received on board, are in fact young men, before they become eligible for licence at the age of eighteen or twenty. Being vicious and ill-disposed, their example is injurious to the younger boys. This state of things points to urgent need of a separation of classes of children in Reformatory schools according to age and character, which at present is impossible. When Reformatory boys prove too much for those in authority, it is very desirable that they should be sent to a school with a discipline of a somewhat more penal character, and more qualified to deal with boys of this order."

In spite of extra precautions and tightening up of discipline, the mischievous state of affairs continued throughout the winter and into 1888, with much insubordination, defiance of officers and frequent abscondings. There was a further setback on November 2nd when the ship broke adrift from her south moorings in a heavy gale and collided with the Conway, resulting in a claim for damages. The Akbar was docked in Birkenhead while her moorings were repaired, and the New Ferry Company sent in a bill for 30/- for services rendered by the SS Firefly during the gale. An extra watch was maintained while she was in dock to cut off the more convenient escape route for the mercurial lads!

Some ship's biscuit and a clog were thrown at one of the instructors who, being unable to trace the culprit screened by the other boys, mustered all the boys on deck, where they were forced to stand to attention for three hours. Two boys who wrenched the clock off the main deck and threw it overboard were punished with 18 cuts of the cane and two days in the cell. A boy of bad character was refused admittance owing to the unsettled situation on board ship.

On January 2nd 1888, when there were 146 boys on board, the Superintendent received a tip that serious violence was intended by the boys on visiting day. The River and Cheshire police were alerted and placed in readiness to board at the first hint of trouble. It was noted "the precaution so cowed the boys that no disturbance took place." Two weeks later, 13 lads absconded in dense fog. They became lost and were rescued by a passing ship. After spending a week in prison on remand, nine were sentenced to three months hard labour and the remainder returned to the Akbar for severe punishment.

It had all been too much for Captain Edwin C Symons RN, who, although he had been exonerated from any blame in connection with the mutiny, had decided to resign his command. His successor, Captain Edward Hicks RN, entered upon his duties in April 1888 at a salary of £300 a year and £42 6s for rations, with residence on ship and gradually restored order and discipline after sporadic outbursts of trouble.

Order Restored

By July there was an indication that matters were finally

improving. Reporting one lad called Donohue, caught in the act of breaking into his cabin, the Captain noted with satisfaction that "the conduct of the other boys who would have dealt with him roughly if permitted, proves that the general feeling is at present strongly opposed to such conduct."

HM Inspector Colonel Inglis summed up the situation at the end of the year: "I found the ship restored to its old condition of peace and obedience, and all promising well. The boys are under firm and kindly discipline. There is a good tone prevailing with no indication now of discomfort or ill-feeling. On the contrary, I found officers and boys working together and all going on well. The ship has entirely recovered its old form, and is now under careful, firm and judicious management...I examined the starboard watch. 24 in standard five: a most intelligent class; work excellent, not one failure; 20 in navigation class; 32 standard four, reading and spelling very good; writing excellent; two failed in dictation; all passed arithmetic. 22 in standard three, very creditable work. 12 in standard two, 4 dunces here. 7 in standard one, fair results. Conduct excellent. Boys mostly ordered and eager to please."

Future flareups were quickly doused. In August 1892, the Captain reported a disturbance on board. "I visited the sleeping deck at about 10pm and was surprised to find a good deal of whistling and insubordinate shouting which the Chief Officer was unable to stop. I was very surprised to hear that it had been going for over half an hour and that I had not been informed. The moment I was on the Deck there was most perfect silence but when I left

Left to right: Officers' training ship HMS Conway, reformatory ship Akbar and the Indefatigable, an orphanage for the education of poor boys

there was a light noise which ceased the moment I returned and was not repeated during the night. The noise resumed at 6.45am and as I could not fix it on any individual, I at once filed the boys on the upper deck and kept them at 'attention' for two hours and cancelled all leave. The usual routine was then proceeded with and the work done in a willing and orderly manner. At noon, two Petty Officers asked permission to address me on behalf of the boys and reported that the boys promised that if leave was resumed there would be no more noise. I at once assembled the whole of the boys and told them I would make no terms, that the leave would be stopped as long as I thought fit and that I would have order and discipline maintained as well. Privately I took all precautions necessary in case of fire or to defeat force if necessary."

By 1900, smoking accounted for much of the punishment on board. The Captain reported: "Our record of punishment would be so much lighter if it were not for the extraordinary passion for cigarette smoking among young boys. The cigarettes they smoke contain filth of the vilest description, and can be bought for ten a penny. They do incalculable harm both physically and morally. I do not believe that we at all realise the mischief that is being done to our children by this vicious habit."

A Dangerous Climate

There were many days in winter when fog blanketed out the Mersey scene, and the wail of the distant fog horns and the repeated echo of the Akbar fog bell were the only sounds to fracture the eerie stillness. At such times the ship was gloomy and many a nervous boy swore he had seen the ghostly outline of a former seaman lurking in the shadows out of range of the old oil lamps. It was on April 6th, 1905, that the lamps were replaced with acetylene gas at a cost of £143 10s. The atmosphere on board immediately became brighter and more cheerful and the menacing apparitions seen by the timorous disappeared. Electric lighting was installed in the Akbar and Farm School in March 1913.

Dense fog on December 30th 1888 prevented the Lord Bishop of Liverpool from boarding to attend the boys' prize distribution, and many of the visitors who had travelled out on an earlier boat for this special occasion were unable to leave and had to spend the night on board. Those who attempted to return to shore could not find the Rock Ferry slip in order to land but "providentially made a good hit of the 'Orion' Light Ship, where, with the boat crew, they remained until the next morning." It was agreed that in future "Prize Day" should be arranged at an earlier date when the weather would be less severe.

Fog was not the only problem; some of the visitors found themselves shipwrecked when gale force winds churned up the Mersey into mountainous breakers. One such incident was reported under the headline "A Shocking Adventure", in the March 1884 issue of the "Reformatory and Refuge Journal":

"A dreadful story of suffering was revealed at an inquest held at Frodsham on the body of a young man named Duckworth, who had come from Blackburn to see his brother, a lad on board the reformatory ship 'Akbar'. At four o'clock a crew of 12 boys, in charge of the coxswain, were about to land two officers, the boy Duckworth, and the letters, when they were caught by a sudden gale. After gallantly struggling for an hour and a half, they found themselves being gradually carried up the Mersey, past Bromborough and Eastham, on the Cheshire shore. Luckily they were in charge of the stoutest boat on board the Akbar, or they would have been inevitably drowned as the waves repeatedly dashed over, drenching them to the skin.

No less than 8 out of the 12 available oars were broken in the terrible struggle against wind and tide. To add to their misery the night became pitch dark and the boat was completely at the mercy of the waves. Four hours later the boat was washed close in shore on the desolate Frodsham Marsh, situated between Frodsham and Ellesmere Port. By wading breast high in water they managed to reach the shore in the most exhausted and forlorn condition. They were without a particle of food, and were almost perished with hunger and cold. Under the advice of the officer in charge, all the lads kept close together to live out the night. The wind swept across the bleak and desolate marsh with terrific fury, bringing on the icy blast of hail, which cut up the lads' hands and faces in a shocking manner. A little later on, Duckworth was found to be missing, and despite the shouts and calls, which were unfortunately drowned by the roar of the gale, nothing further was seen of him until daylight broke upon the miserable group. To get off the marsh is impossible at night, it being several thousand acres in extent, and intersected at every hundred yards by wide and deep dykes full of water. There is not a stick or tree upon it, and here for 10 hours through that awful night the poor boys bore the full brunt of the storm. One by one they succumbed to sleep, and were with difficulty roused by their comrades in misery. When day dawned, despite every exertion, four had fallen apparently dying. The chief officer set off to obtain assistance. Unfortunately, no conveyance could reach the spot, and the helpless, almost lifeless lads, had to be carried a mile and a half to Frodsham, where they were put to bed in the Queen's Head Inn, and every attention was paid to them by the medical men of the town. In the meantime, searchers were looking for Duckworth, and he was soon discovered about a quarter of a mile from the spot where the lads had fought out the gale, lying on his side cold and stiff, having perished from exposure. The officer in his evidence told the coroner and jury that they would never forget the awful agonising experience during the storm all night to which they were exposed, without food or shelter, for fourteen hours. The coroner said the fact that any of the boys survived the terrible exposure spoke highly of their stamina, and the treatment they received on board the Akbar. The Jury returned a verdict of death from exposure."

Mr Allen, the Instructor, who lost his teeth in the disaster, was granted five guineas for a replacement set.

All the year round hazards were revealed in various entries in the old Minute Books. "March 1867: In consideration of many services rendered to us by the Rock Ferry Company, it has been decided not to press a claim for damages to the galley when run into by the steamer 'Bee'." "1886: Captain reported the 'Great Eastern' to be anchored in a dangerous position to the ship Akbar. Owners were warned that they would be held responsible for any damage and the Admiralty informed." "1887: Offensive smell from the cargo of 'Locksley Hall', nuisance and source of danger to health of those living on board. Dock Board reports they will do everything to remove cargo with least possible delay." "1887: During a violent gale ship parted from her moorings and breaking adrift was driven on the mud between New and Rock Ferry slipway."

The lifespan of the ageing Akbar was lengthened by constant repairs and renewals, carried out in the main by the ship's carpenter. A master craftsman, he was responsible for all repairs and building and proved his worth as one of the most valued men on board. When dry rot threatened the stern of the ship in 1872, it was Mr Wilkinson, the ship's carpenter, who cleared out the rotten wood and filled the gaping cavity with a ton and a half of rock salt. In that year he renewed the front part of the poop, extending it four feet to protect the tanks and pipes of the hot water apparatus; built a new cutter, repaired the skylights to the galley and the lift, and made new wooden baths for washing facilities. In 1878, the carpenter weatherproofed the upper deck by sheeting it with two-inch planking, and in 1889 he improved the accommodation on the orlop deck to create more space and ventilation for the boys who slept there in hammocks. In that year too he created a new water closet for the Captain, who had complained to the Committee: "My water closet is 80-years-old and on the side of the ship, and during a storm proves quite dangerous to use." Each winter the topsail yards were downed and the top masts struck.

Diet and Health

In the early days the ship's water supply presented many problems. At the start, the Akbar boats ferried the water in containers from Tranmere, each trip with ten tons of water costing £4. In 1863, a new pump was fitted to make more efficient the collection of rainwater. By 1879, the water was delivered to the ship at a service charge of £45 yearly plus 2/6d per 1,000 gallons. Captain Hicks complained in 1894 that "Liverpool is certainly the only large Port in the world where there is no public water boat." By 1900, Birkenhead Corporation was making a charge of 3/- per 1,000 gallons.

The boys were always hungry in those early days. The food they ate, although considered adequate, contributed little towards their bodily warmth. In the winter months they were continuously chilled, and whenever the opportunity arose for a lad to snatch an extra ship's biscuit, he would gladly risk his punishment of 18 strokes across his backside.

Food was locked away and it was a puzzle in April 1864 as to how Matthew, one of the 203 boys on board, managed to obtain and hungrily wolf down a great deal of porridge. So unaccustomed was his stomach to food in such quantity that the lad collapsed and died! The body was handed over to his mother for burial.

Meat was an expensive item and there was consternation among the Committee in 1871 when the supplier reported that he was compelled to raise his meat prices from $7\frac{1}{4}$d to $7\frac{1}{2}$d!

HM Inspector complained in 1875: "The boys are not very robust and there have been three deaths in the year. Salt beef, soup and biscuit comprise too large a part of the dietary. I recommend two or three slices of fresh cooked meat in the week, more bread instead of biscuits, and a supply of potatoes and vegetables." Five years later the boys were being given soft bread twice a week. In 1895, they received a 2 ounce smear of margarine four times instead of twice a week, and a meat dinner to replace one dinner of bread and cheese. The possibility that they should have milk in their tea and coffee was deferred for further consideration. Breakfast then consisted of 4 ounces of biscuit with porridge.

HM Inspector reported in 1904: "The boys in the mass look far from well. There are too many puffy pasty faces and skin eruptions. The boys are being dosed with lime juice, but what is wanted is not the means to deal with trouble when it does arise, but measures to forestall the trouble." Under his watchful eye, the situation gradually improved with the addition of fresh fish twice a week, doses of cod liver oil, vegetables, and in 1914, the feast of bread and scouse dinners! By 1924, the results of the more satisfactory balanced diet were reflected in the quarterly reports showing weight increases of three pounds a lad and a growth in height of half an inch, with the observation that "the boys are now looking healthy and stout."

Extremes of temperature were felt more severely on board the Akbar than in any of the shore schools. The suffering from the elements in winter was acute, with chilblains, diseases of respiratory organs, consumption, pneumonia and asthma. Colds, influenza and hacking coughs spread like wildfire among both lads and staff in the cramped confined area, so that infections at times debilitated 50% of those on board. Ventilation on the sleeping deck as late as 1904 was appalling, especially in winter when ports could not be opened as freely as in fine weather. In summer, the boys were berthed midships in a sort of sweat box but even this discomfort was preferable to the horrendous cold of 1894, the year Queen Victoria opened the Manchester Ship Canal. The weather in that winter was so severe that the Canal remained frozen for about 13 weeks, and some of the river as well.

In an effort to keep out the chill the boys were fed oatmeal gruel before bedtime and had their calico shirts replaced by jersey frocks. Deaths on board were not uncommon, with as many as six in one year, and four in others, usually the result of consumption, pneumonia, pleurisy and brain disease. In 1896, a nurse hired from the Women's Hospital lived on the ship to care for the seriously ill. "I am sorry to say your nephew/son is very ill and sinking fast" - many such messages were despatched to relatives. The Committee at one stage seriously considered buying a private burial plot before deciding it would be more economical to bury the lads in a public grave at a cost of 12/6d a body. There were serious cases of typhoid and osteomyelitis, and minor cases of scalds, broken limbs, hernias and housemaid's knee. During the annual painting of the ship, "painter's colic" (lead poisoning) was an additional problem. In 1915, 234 boys had diarrhoea, and the Medical Officer recommended a more suitable store place for the meat supply.

In December 1894, when smallpox broke out on the Clarence, all the Akbar boys were vaccinated at a cost of 1/- each. There was so much sickness in Liverpool in 1865 that Captain Borland suspended all leave. Epidemics of sickness and a wave of smallpox and cholera ashore frequently left the ship in isolation.

Staff often requested leave to "recoup my health", and the failing health of others forced them to resign. Typical examples

Both of the Liverpool Catholic Reformatory Association ships, each named Clarence, came to catastrophic ends when they were deliberately set on fire by some of the inmates. Clarence (the second), pictured here, remained in the Sloyne, off New Ferry, between November 1885 and July 1899.

were the Chaplain and the Chief Officer who quit in 1860. In 1866, the Schoolmaster moved on for "a change of air", and in the year following the Bandmaster stated that, in consequence of the damp cold state of the orlop deck, he would not be able to remain on board another winter. Captain Borland resigned in 1868, because "my ill health will not permit another winter on board," and his replacement, Captain Urmston RN from Kingussie, Inverness, accepted the £300 per annum plus £42 6s allowance position on the understanding that he would not bring his wife and family on board until after the winter months. A year later he was dead of "congestion of the lungs brought on by typhoid fever." All applicants for the position of Captain were told: "The post is not an easy one. It requires tact, knowledge of character, patience and habits of order and the Committee will not consider it right to appoint and retain anyone who does not conduct the duties of the Vessel in a successful as well as a diligent manner." They might well have added the importance of a strong constitution!

In 1893 a grievous attack of pleuro-pneumonia which assumed an infectious character brought the following criticism from HM Inspector: "The one weak point in the ship is her record of sickness. The fact that health on board during the past ten years, as judged by the vital statistics, does not appear to be up to the level of other ships, demands the careful consideration of the Committee."

This censure resulted in action and the boys were despatched for a fortnight's holiday to the Cholera Hospital at New Ferry, empty at the time and loaned by the Liverpool Corporation. In their absence all the decayed wood of the Akbar was replaced and the ship thoroughly fumigated, cleaned, ventilated and lime-washed throughout. Reported the Captain: "The result of the experiment was most successful, not only has the condition of the ship been improved but the boys benefitted greatly from the change and the run in the grass field during the magnificent weather. Relaxation of discipline was unavoidable in such a place but the lads could not have behaved better and in no instance did they take advantage of the almost absolute freedom. They returned in the best of health and spirits."

Bed-wetting was a problem. In 1858, Captain Fenwick was ordered to refuse admission to any boys with this tendency, and the Gaol Warder informed that it was his duty to report all such cases to the Medical Officer. Nevertheless, boys with this weakness were always on board, and in 1863 there were 31 recorded cases. Boys who soiled their cloth blanket were deprived of water. This inhuman attempt to control the nuisance was hell in high summer for thirsty lads enduring a heat which frequently zoomed to the level of a Turkish bath! Physical punishment included flogging and caning. Henry was so fearful of his chastisement in August 1872 that he clambered down to the bottom of the accommodation ladder in the still of the night, and whilst attempting to wash out his blanket before official inspection, overbalanced and fell into the Mersey. His body was never found.

The problem was nationwide and in the more enlightened and sympathetic days of March 1926, it was discussed at length at a Home Office Schools' Conference. Doctor Norris blamed bad ventilation, constipation, adenoids and unclean beds and told those who attended that other causes included "Dormitories that are often very cold, and in such cases when the child is moved to a well heated school hospital, the bed wetting ceases; on bath nights, when there is an increase in the number of bed wetters, brought on by the sudden cold of the water." He advised that windows should be closed one hour before retiring and opened after the children were put to bed; that each child should have a mackintosh, preferably red, over which should be placed a thin blanket, and once only, on the hour after retiring, should the children be called to empty their bladders. Wet-bed dormitories which had hard boards as beds should be abolished. He stated that children who feared punishment for bed-wetting became over-anxious and unable to control themselves, and he advised every Medical Officer to examine every child carefully for worms, kidney or bladder disease.

There was no sympathy or understanding for children of weak habits, particularly for those who indulged in masturbation. Reported the Captain in 1872: "Smith who is nearly blind through bad habits is being kept in the sick bay for security and put in a straight jacket." Epileptic lads and those with lunatic tendencies were discharged and more often than not despatched to the workhouse. Such a case was Saville in 1886, whose discharge the Superintendent recommended, stating, "he is daft and unfit for industrial training." A problem lad who, after trying to drown himself, hid away in the hope that he would die of starvation was discharged on the grounds that he was too much of a problem.

A dentist was appointed in 1861 and there were several examples of boys absconding in preference to treatment. Toothbrushes were introduced in 1913. Other improvements over the years included separate towels in 1863, to avoid the rapid spread of inflamed eyes which had resulted in nine of the 154 boys on board being taken to hospital. In 1893, there were straw beds in the sick bay and bread and milk for the patients; in 1905 knives and forks instead of spoons; in 1906, collapsible beds instead of hammocks; in 1922, undergarments were supplied and in 1924 shoes, to relieve continued use of boots. Strict hygiene regulations were later imposed by HM Inspectors to wipe out infection and each evening the order of the day was: "Last post and gargle!"

End of an Era

By the turn of the century anxiety regarding the ship's worsening condition was justified. Several leaks were stemmed to no avail, and by 1906 the Akbar was making a ton of water every 24 hours. As the pounding of the Mersey tides took its toll, it became obvious to all concerned that the days of the old ship were numbered.

A final repair to the ship's side at a cost of £2 10s was attempted but the ship still continued to make a great deal of water through her bottom. Captain Powley reported that he did not consider it safe to rig the main sail again, and Messrs Clover, Clayton & Company recommended the use of Condy's fluid to disinfect the objectionable ooze in the ship's midst.

Captain Hicks had reported in 1900, "Over 2,500 boys have passed through the Akbar since her establishment forty-six years ago, and we know from official returns that 23 of these were under detention in prison in 1900. This is less than one per cent. The respectable appearance of the old lads who have visited the ship and who have been otherwise heard of is the best evidence of the success of our work. In the many letters I have received from old boys, kindly reference is made to the Akbar. It is a good sign when boys speak well of their old school."

By 1906, fifty years after the first boys came to the Akbar, the number of admissions had increased to 3,177. Of these: 127 died,

The last days of the Akbar. One of the picturesque features of the Mersey for over a quarter of a century, the Akbar in November 1907, a month before being towed to the breaker's yard

87 were transferred, 1,787 sent to sea, 286 to other employment, 381 returned to family or friends, 33 enlisted, 14 emigrated, 61 absconded, 4 were sent to prison, 78 were discharged on account of disease and 25 by special warrant. 312 were under detention in December 1906.

The Akbar remained in use until Monday December 2nd 1907, when the old sailing ship, unable to weather any further service, was towed away to the breaker's yard. The school transferred to Heswall on the Wirral, under the new title of a Nautical Training School, where it continued to function until its closure in 1956.

The Akbar had broken a few hearts and spirits with discipline which at times chilled the entire hulk, and she had claimed a fair number of deaths, but for many she had provided a one-way ticket to a decent life, considerable success and the chance, for some, to slot into the comfortable confident strata of the middle classes. As the lads rowed ashore for the last time on that cold December morning, there were more than a few who took a backward glance at the outline of the crippled and dying hulk through misty eyes. It was the end of an era for floating reformatories.

Clarence boys proudly displaying their uniform (1895-99)

The Clarence

The initial progress of the Liverpool Juvenile Reformatory Association was closely monitored by leading Catholics in the town. In 1858, whilst on a visit to Liverpool and much to the surprise of local Catholics, Cardinal Wiseman suggested a fact-finding visit to the Akbar. He was accompanied by the Bishop of Shrewsbury, whose diocese included the South Bank of the Mersey, and many of the clergy, all of whom received a warm welcome from the Akbar committee of managers, highly gratified by their interest.

The first annual meeting of the Liverpool Catholic Reformatory Association was in 1864 when Father James Nugent, revered for his tireless work for waifs and strays and the poor of the city, was made president. A proposal to establish a Ship Reformatory in the Sloyne, off New ferry, had already been agreed and the Lords of the Admiralty were persuaded to loan a suitable man-of-war for this purpose. Her Majesty's ship Clarence, an 84-gun line-of-battle ship of 2,279 tons register, launched in July 1827 and called after the Duke of Clarence, at that time Lord of the Admiralty, began her new role on 15th August 1864. She could accommodate at least 250 boys, but was rarely filled to capacity. The curriculum and timetable on board was similar to that of the Akbar, with the majority of the boys being taken into the Merchant Service.

The ship came to a catastrophic end on the night of January 17th 1884, when a few boys set fire to her. In spite of the frantic efforts of Dock Board officials, the Liverpool Corporation and volunteers, she was completely burnt out with all equipment and stores. Fortunately no lives were lost, and the six boys responsible for the fire were sent to the Assizes and sentenced to five years penal servitude.

The Clarence boys were temporarily housed in the Port Sanitary Hospital at Bebington, until a threatened outbreak of cholera in Liverpool forced the Health Committee to resume occupation of the premises, and at 24 hours' notice the school was moved to a land-based reformatory.

The committee of the Clarence appealed to the Admiralty for the loan of another ship. The Admiralty, naturally apprehensive after the previous loss, replied with a demand that first the insurance money should be paid over to them. When told that the hard-up committee had only insured for the amount necessary to outfit another ship, the Admiralty insisted that the loan of another ship would depend on the committee's ability to insure the hulk against fire. It was some time before a company could be found to accept such an obvious risk. The Admiralty claimed the proceeds of the sale of the wreckage salvage, which amounted to £1,509, before finally agreeing that the 120-gun Royal William, launched in 1828, could be renamed the Clarence in her new role as a floating reformatory. All the delays meant that the ship did not come into commission until November 1885.

The committee decided for better discipline and the former Merchant Service Captain resigned and was replaced by a Royal Navy officer, Captain E P Statham. The boys challenged the new tough regime early in February 1886, with a serious mutiny, which ended in 13 of the ringleaders going to the Assizes. On the previous evening 10 boys planning to abscond were locked up for the night. Next morning they refused sullenly to obey orders and were joined by three others. The leader, named Scully, armed himself with a long sharp knife, and the rest with belaying pins, broken oars and lengths of wood. Two senior boys and officers who intervened were attacked, and helpers urgently summoned from shore had their boats capsized by boats from the Clarence being manhandled over the side to crash down on top of them.

The ringleaders threatened to kill the captain, who was below decks and centred their fury on Frederick Potter, head school-master, who received three head wounds and was so badly stabbed that he nearly died. At this point the captain (nick-named "Hot Soup" by the boys) came on the scene and threatened the mutineers with an old pistol, for which he had in fact no ammunition. The boys gave themselves up. The 13 ringleaders went to the Assizes, where Scully got 5 years penal servitude and the rest 12 months hard labour.

Captain G H Yonge, RN, followed Captain Statham in 1895, and

Instructors and staff on board the Clarence. They had to be "persons of sober life and conversation, and free from drunken-ness, profane cursing and swearing, lewdness and other dissolute immoral or disorderly practices".

lived on board with his wife and three young daughters. Peace reigned until the early morning of 26th July 1899, when the end came with disastrous finality. The Clarence was set ablaze by some boys after weeks of concealed preparation carrying oily waste down into the bowels of the ship. The fire was planned for the very night the Bishop of Shrewsbury was on board in preparation for a Confirmation service the next morning. The Bishop and the 235 boys and staff were got away safely. However, the fire spread so quickly that nothing could be saved, and at 6.00am the ship broke her back and sank. The survivors possessed nothing but the clothes they were wearing. The Catholic Reformatory Association then finished with floating reformatories and established a nautical training school on dry land, St Aidan's, which remained at Farnworth, near Widnes, until its closure in 1981.

For boys not robust enough for sea training, the Catholic Reformatory Association set up a land reformatory to supplement the work of the Clarence. The Birkdale Farm School opened on 9th March 1872, with Captain Joseph Smith of the 7th Fusiliers as Superintendent. Captain Smith was recalled to the army in November 1876 and was followed by Daniel Henry Shee, who ruled successfully for 30 years. The title changed to St Thomas More School in 1933 and was so called until December 1984, when the school closed to be reopened as a centre for psychiatric rehabilitation.

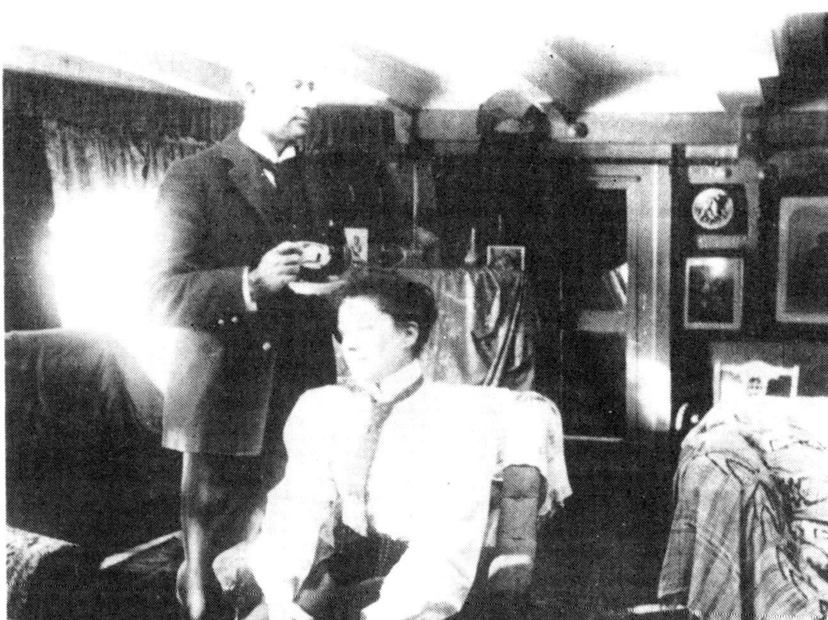

Captain G H Yonge RN takes a break for a cup of tea with Mrs Yonge in his dining room

THE GIRLS

A Woman's Place

In those far-off days of mid-Victorian England, woman power was a big joke. The male ruled unequivocally. The majority of women were humiliated, abused, underprized, and worked as hard as the weary horses that pulled much of the traffic of the day, and as far as men were concerned, they were comparable in intellect. Few women complained; indeed, to do so would have been to invite the awesome wrath not only of their husband but of his friends and family, united in their commiseration for a man who had had the misfortune to marry a woman with an opinion of her own and the spirit to express it.

The press idealised the drudgery, in comments like that of Saturday, April 23rd, 1853, on the "Role of Englishwomen and their value to society."

"How well and pleasantly they serve in shops; how cheerfully they clean and keep order in our houses; how exquisitely they get up our shirts and mend our stockings; how well they dress our beef steaks and mash the potatoes; how joyfully they sing at their spinning wheels and tend their cows.
"What admirable daughters to our small agriculture and tradesmen; what mothers to our soldiers and sailors.
"How handsome too, fresh coloured and beaming with healthful beauty and guided by that straight forward hardy sort of intellect which knows how to make the best - even of a bad husband and not being ashamed of being a woman."

Opportunities for women to augment their scanty living were limited to the most menial and harsh of tasks. An illustration is in a reader's letter to the local press in 1872: "This very year, Parliament is expected to pass the Metalliferous Mines Act which will deny hundreds of women and children the right to augment their family income by simple underground tasks."

The gentlemen of the Liverpool Reformatory Association were equally as prejudiced and it was not until June 1916, three years before British women got the vote, and after considerable correspondence with a less bigoted HM Inspector of Reformatories, that they were persuaded to elect a woman to their Committee. The ultimate accolade went to a Miss E Blease, who had for a number of years been a visitor to the girls' home to encourage the matron and generally supervise the house and the employment and instruction of the inmates. Her appointment was not a unanimous decision and there remained on the Committee members firmly convinced that for a woman to become involved in any political process was the most effective way to assure her equality, and this was something they hoped would never happen.

In short, women were expected to be perfect housewives and

mothers, to work like slaves or be decorative according to their station in society, and nothing more. It followed that those who failed to live up to these standards were severely censured and this was reflected in the stern treatment of the girls in the Reformatory Home.

A Measure of Success

Number 6 Mount Vernon Green, a rambling private house situated on high ground at Edge Hill with open views front and back, was bought for £1,500 from Mr James Addam in the spring of 1857 for its new function as a girls' reformatory. Its first registered owner was in residence in 1754, and the building's condition reflected its age. To make it habitable for between 50 and 60 girls, £198 was spent on alterations, repairs, fittings, and sewers at 7/6d a yard, 8 feet below the bottom of the garden. The dormitories were far too small to accommodate the large number of girls and the one situated in what had been the hay loft had the added disadvantage of a leaking roof.

Mrs Wilson was appointed matron at a salary of £70 a year with coals, gas and washing. A furnished sitting room and bedroom went with the appointment but she had to provide food for herself and family. The salary remained virtually the same for many years and indeed in 1898, when a Miss Laurie was recruited for the same job, her salary was quoted as being £65 a year with an allowance of £23 8s in lieu of rations. Miss Townsend, the assistant teacher, was paid £15 a year at the outset, the same as Hannah Kirby, the cook and general servant.

Between 1857 and 1921 several thousand girls passed through the portals of Mount Vernon Green and its associate establishment, Toxteth Park Girls' Reformatory, under the vigilant eye of the Liverpool Reformatory Association. In 1897 they were described as "very unpromising material" by Her Majesty's Inspector of Reformatories.

On May 13th 1880 Inspector Major Inglis had also noted in his inspection report:
"The girls are taken from a class which is familiar with criminal practice and immoral living. The life, from day to day, under the discipline of the school, and in spite of strong and earnest efforts for self improvement, gives evidence of what lies beneath the surface, and of the strong passions more or less kept under control. During the past year there have been outbreaks of evil tendency and inclinations reverting to acts of theft, lying, disobedience, rudeness and impropriety.
"The inmates seem to be drawn from a still lower stratum than ever before and are very unpromising materials. To raise such a class from the depth of depravity and utter neglect in which they have been sunk, is indeed a work of Christian charity and mercy; but it is one of labour and difficulty, and only a certain amount of success can be anticipated.
"The school continues to maintain its reputation. It deals with

the roughest material possible, and effects perhaps as much practically as can be achieved with such objects to work upon. Generally the girls who are brought within its influences have previously passed through every phase of degradation, and it is no light effort to induce a sense of responsibility.
"The difficulties in carrying on such a school as this are very great; they can only be overcome by the exercise of great patience and forbearance, by much self-denial and command of temper, combined with experience of the class of girls which are to be dealt with, and sound practical common sense. I see these qualities at work in this school in a very large measure. The results are beyond one's sober expectations."

The transformation of a succession of rough, vulgar, illiterate and roguish girls into material worthy of a respectable marital station in life was no easy task for the Liverpool reformers. The Superintendent's register showed by 1873 that 109 of the girls discharged from the school had married "most satisfactorily and respectably", reflecting the permanent effect of the influence gained over them and proving for the reformers the true measure of their success.

For the annual treat at the school on the first Monday of each new year, the old girls were invited back for tea and bun-loaf and to collect their 10/- reward money for producing either their marriage certificate or proof that they had remained in the same situation for 12 months.

Mrs Dearl, the matron, reported with pride on the 1885 treat: "There were present 48 old girls, 34 in service and the 14 married who brought their marriage lines for us to see. They all looked most respectable and were well behaved and orderly. One girl brought her bank book, showing £5 entered in her account. I think this will stimulate others to save. One girl had remained in her first situation for six years and several from one to four years."

"We have received a most grateful letter from a girl who emigrated to America, thanking us for all that had been done for her whilst in ths school and expressing her willingness to assist any others who might be sent out. Several ladies in Canada are willing to pay the passage money if we can recommend good girls. It is a splendid chance for many of our girls who are anxious to get right away from their old surroundings.
"Two other girls who emigrated to America have written encouraging letters speaking most gratefully of the 'old home', as they call the school."

The fortunate few who became esteemed members of the well-to-do middle class, however, ended all connections with the old school. Girls like Alice, who married a ship's captain, and Letitia, whose husband was a prosperous businessman with a fine house, carriage and pair, and a staff to obey all her commands, did not wish embarrassing secrets of youthful errors to be remembered. In 1904, when the doors of opportunity for women were slightly more ajar and several old girls had become matrons of convalescent homes, Miss Phillips, who was then matron of the Liverpool Girls' Reformatory, commented sadly: "It is painful to feel that, owing to the bitterness of the world against reformatories, many of our most successful girls find that it is better to keep secret their connection with a reformatory. A change in the name of our school seems desirable." Fifteen months later the title "Reformatory" was replaced with "Girls' Training Home". But in spite of the change of name, there were many who preferred to close the chapter for ever.

Fallen Women

It was sad, but typical of the era, that as far as the Liverpool Reformatory Association was concerned the girls were second class citizens and in their eyes a delinquent girl was far more offensive than a miscreant lad.

It was noted in the minutes of September 21st 1880 that the number of girls sent to reformatories was not nearly so large as the number of boys, yet the Secretary believed that everyone who had anything to do with reformatories would agree that the girls were much more difficult to reform than the boys, and the girls were in need of more moral care and protection than the boys. The Victorians were obsessed with fallen women.

Many of the homes for girl orphans in 1868 carried the proviso that children admitted must be "innocent", and this rule also applied to the Industrial Schools' Certificate about the same time, which stated categorically that "any children admitted through this channel must be innocent." After some years the supply from this source diminished to such a degree that the certificate was abandoned.

In 1876 there were 6,816 females and 6,501 males in Walton Prison. One in six of the women were in prison for the first time, the majority having succumbed to moral temptation. On the surface, English society in the latter half of the nineteenth century was refined and righteous, and those who succumbed received little sympathy.

The horror of bearing an illegitimate child led to a high suicide rate among unmarried mothers and appalling tragedies followed attempts to abort their misfortune and so avoid Victorian denunciation. Nevertheless, back-street abortionists flourished on the shillings scraped together by the sad, desperate girls fearing the condemnation of society.

Infanticide through neglect was a regular occurrence; the bodies of newly born babies were dumped in back street gutters, ashpits or in the river, with verdicts of "Murder against some person unknown" their only epitaph.

A girl's tragic period of wretchedness began when she realised that she was about to become an unmarried mother. Disowned by her family, condemned as an outcast by the community, and often penniless, her only hope of help was to give birth in the overcrowded union workhouse. Several of the reformatory girls who returned from licence in an "unfortunate way", and unwanted by family and friends, were sent to the workhouse by the Liverpool reformers.

"April 5th 1880. Emma returned from her situation on January 12th for impudent conduct has since been found to be pregnant. HM Inspector Rogers recommends application for her discharge in view of getting her into a lying-in hospital or her own parish workhouse for her confinement and subsequently placing her out in some farm house."

"Sarah re-admitted on 25th February 1880 in an unfortunate condition. Apply for her discharge she to be removed to West Derby workhouse for her confinement." Four months later: "Sarah absconds from workhouse". The babies were usually sent to orphanages.

Medical care outside the workhouse was rough and unsympathetic. On December 18th 1861 a three-day-old baby died from the effects of essence of peppermint and castor oil, which had been given to it by a woman who was attending upon the mother, and was ignorant of its probable effect. Some pregnant girls were sent to mental hospitals, where they encountered formidable restrictions reflecting the stern disapproval of the governing bodies. "Lunatics and Idiots allowed visitors," read the notice posted on

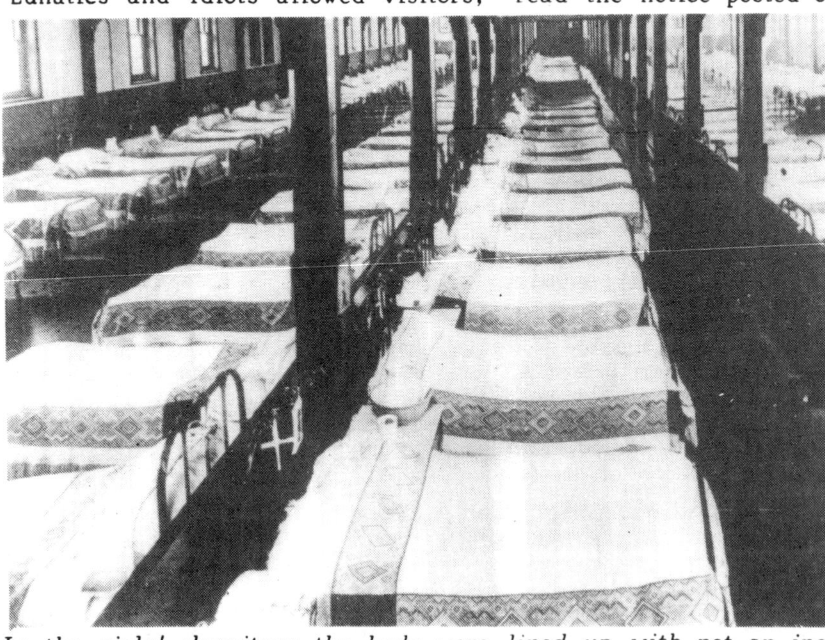

In the girls' dormitory the beds were lined up with not an inch to spare between each, and with as many as 120 girls sharing the one sleeping room. (Delinquent girls' school, Ford)

the wall. Unmarried mothers were not permitted visitors. The combination of pain and guilt from bearing an illegitimate child also resulted in a fair number of the unfortunate girls being sent to the lunatic asylum as long-term inmates.

Pregnant and immoral girls were frequently banished to a penitentiary to spend many hours on their knees in devout prayer asking the Lord to forgive the error of their ways. A penitentiary at Chester reported to the Administrative Diocesan Committee in 1880: "Four girls have been discharged, two of whom are truly penitent." The attitude of the Church to adoption at that time was one of opposition and any attempt to legalise adoption was thwarted as encouraging promiscuity. Indeed, England was one of the last countries to have adoption laws, with the first Adoption Act introduced as late as 1926.

A few voices in the wilderness tried to help and some attempts were made to raise funds for mother and baby homes. One of the most remarkable women to throw in her support was the Mayoress of Southport, Mrs L S Booth, who in 1898 bravely told a public meeting:

"It is a tragedy that women have to bear the whole of the shame. The partners in their sin ought to be the partners in their sorrow. Legislation should be so arranged as to make both parties take equal responsibility, and parents should teach their sons that a woman should be as sacred to them as their mother or sister." Mrs Booth was way ahead of her time and her comments created newspaper headlines and after dinner conversation for many a day.

Immoral girls were a headache for the reformers. The problem was aired in a letter from the Chairman of the Liverpool Committee to HM Inspector the Reverend Sydney Turner, who replied thus: "December 29th 1873. My Dear Sir; I regret to be unable to give you any advice on this matter. I cannot in fact make out any 'Law or Rule' as to this vicious class of girls by which one can be guided. There is little doubt that the majority of girls sent to reformatory schools at and after 14 years of age are familiar with vice and have more or less practised it. On the other hand very many of these are reformed and some who are admitted of the innocent sort, fall away when on licence, or after discharge, while the others hold fast to the better way they have learned and entered on. Besides it is remarkable that in our most successful Reformatory (Ipswich) such vicious or vice-stained cases are commonly received and form the majority in the school."

"I am afraid that we must be content to do what we can for exciting better feelings and ingraining better tastes and habits and then leave the work and its results to the issue of time and circumstances.

"I do not advise however that prostitute cases should be received and I should steadily refuse to admit any who are not certified by the medical authority of the gaol they come from, to be free from venereal disease, and if they were passed on to the school inspite of these precautions under a false or incorrect certificate, I should send them back or apply for their discharge as not eligible under the conditions which have been agreed to.

"If a girl went wrong, on licence, not criminally but viciously I should apply for her discharge and try to get her into some Magdalene asylum. She would do more harm in returning to the school, than the school could do her good. The school is formed and licensed to reform from thievish propensities and not from vice. On the other hand I hope that Mrs Molleson, the matron, won't be too squeamish. In fact I feel sure that she will not let any chance of doing good to anyone escape her when it is fairly placed in her way by the cause of providential circumstances. Wishing you all the blessings of the New Year."

Mrs Molleson continued to prove her worth, aided by a punishment system which permitted any girl guilty of immodesty or indecency to spend three days of solitary confinement in a gloomy cell on a diet of bread and water.

The Committee went to extreme lengths to protect the girls. On hearing, with considerable agitation, that the Volunteers Engineer Corps were about to take over the adjoining property for their quarters, the Secretary wrote strongly to the Commanding Officer, stressing the need to keep his men under firm control, as most of the girls next door were of light virtue and even the mildest of flirtations, such as a wink or a whistle, must be forbidden. As far as the girls were concerned, they were warned that any attempt to coquette would bring them corporal punishment.

The system coped with the sinful until December 1912, when separate accommodation was sought for young girls of suspected or known immoral conduct. "The Willows", next door at number 5 Mount Vernon Green, was opened on January 13th 1913 as a reformatory penitentiary, and licensed for the admission of 10 immoral girls, the number being doubled 12 months later.

Girls like Ada and Fanny, who returned from licence with VD, were sent to the Lock Hospital, maintained by public subscription, where they wore purple dresses and when cured were sent to St Monica's or a similar penitentiary to reflect with contrition on their wickedness and moral corruption.

It was suggested by Mill Road Hospital authorities that Eva, who picked up syphilis and housemaid's knee whilst on licence as a parlourmaid, could remain at school during her six months of treatment. This was rejected and instead the hospital was paid 6/- a week for her maintenance. At the end of that time, Eva was cured of housemaid's knee but still had syphilis and the Committee ordered her discharge from their responsibility.

Education

The education of the reform school girls was not without problems. On May 22nd 1876 an official inspection of Mount

Vernon Green showed there were 83 girls in the school: nine between the ages of 11 and 13; twenty from 13 to 15; and thirteen with ages ranging from 15 to 17. Thirty-three of these had no previous convictions; eight had one previous conviction, and there was one girl with two previous convictions. Twenty-two of the girls could neither read nor write; thirteen imperfectly and seven could read and write well.

Major Inglis reported: "Educationally I found the classes with the exception of the first class, rather backward; most of the girls are well advanced in point of age, and when admitted, as a rule know literally nothing. It is very difficult to move such cases out of their intellectual lethargy. Still the effort should be made, and if the girl is to be raised morally, the school room must not be neglected.

"There is an extensive laundry for the elder girls and the work is carried on vigorously. The younger girls are systematically trained in needlework, cooking, household work and knitting.

"The school continues to maintain its reputation. It deals with the roughest materials possible, and effects perhaps as much practically as can be achieved with such objects to work upon. In the three previous years, 81 girls have been discharged with the majority to service. Fifty-nine are known to be doing well; sixteen unknown; two have died; one girl is bad and doubtful and five have been convicted of crime."

An earlier inspection report noted: "The first class read and answered my questions exceedingly well, showing much serious thought and intelligence; in cyphering and English dictation and spelling, they have done but tolerably. The second class is very backward in reading as well as cyphering, only about half of them being able to make out even easy words or to answer correctly in their tables. The third class is composed mostly of girls lately admitted and ignorant almost of letters. To teach girls such an age as the majority arriving at the present is a very difficult task."

It was a hard battle for the staff, with many resignations and weeks of absence in order to recuperate their health. During the twelve months of 1902 there were five changes of house matron; four of laundry matrons; five of washhouse matrons; three of sewing matrons and one of a schoolmistress who resigned in hysterics after a girl called her "Miss Piggy". In 1903 Miss Collins resigned, finding her duties as house matron too heavy; the sewing matron quit in 1917 because "the hours are too long and I have not sufficient time off duty." A year later the kitchen matron finished because she did not like the basement kitchen.

The staff who remained were martyrs to duty who soon became worn out and an easy prey to the infection which abounded. They were frequently required to double up on duties, the matron to give cookery lessons and the teachers to take drill and singing lessons. Their living conditions left a lot to be desired, as indicated in an Inspector's report in November 1895, which referred to "the poverty of the officers' accommodation and the lowness of the lean-to shed which acts as a wash house." There were complaints of rats, defective drainage, moths in furniture and insects in the straw palliasses of both girls and staff.

The staff were often ill-equipped for the difficult task of teaching unruly and ignorant girls. In 1871, for example, a Miss Collings, "for some time waiting maid to the Duchess of Marlborough", ruled briefly as school mistress. Although battling against tremendous odds, teachers frequently came under fire from HM Inspector, with blame for the girls' scholastic inadequacies.

In 1890 the Inspector noted: "In my opinion a change in the schoolroom is plainly desirable. The results of my examination were very unfavourable. The girls were well behaved and orderly and my only complaint is connected with their education.

"What is wanted is a resolute and earnest teacher, of full control, who will not allow these girls to remain impassive and content, but will stir them up to activity and exertion.

"Some change for the better must be insisted upon. The girls do not get their allotted time in the schoolroom and one teacher is not competent to deal with 80 backward girls. The government rule is that each child should have 15 or 16 hours per week in the schoolroom. The laundry work in this school is carried on vigorously at the expense of the education. Too much of this work is taken in hand, with depressing effect and it takes up a great deal of the girls' time and attention. Care should be taken not to press this class of labour unduly. I would ask the committee to look carefully into the allotment of time for school instruction and labour respectively.

"A time table must be drawn up and adhered to so as to give a fair share of time to the schoolroom as well as to the washroom and laundry.

"The girls work hard, and this labour has its practical value but it should not be carried on at the expense of the moral and intellectual cultivation of the girls. They want more outdoor exercise, and not quite so much devotion to the washing tub. The girls sing well and musical drill has been introduced and I hope it will be kept up; it is the very thing the girls want for they are not very robust."

The Laundry

All the girls made their own clothing, knitted their stockings and carried out all the kitchen and housework. In the main it was the laundry girls, half the total number of the school, who worked the hardest.

Work in the laundry was like slavery, with limited and defective equipment in appalling conditions. The clothes were washed in wooden troughs, replaced by the earthenware kind in 1897, and it was not until 1899 that gas was fitted to the laundry and schoolroom. All the water, described as being "soft and most excellent for washing and boiling peas," had to be heated, and this operation resulted in horrendous accidents, scalds and burns. A victim of the dangers involved was 13-year-old Caroline, one of the girls appointed to look after heating the water for the girls' Saturday baths. In December 1873 a piece of soap slipped down the back of the copper and whilst trying to retrieve it, Caroline stood upon the pieces of loose wood which covered the boiler. The wood cracked and the screaming girl plunged into the boiling water, scalding her legs.

Reported Matron Mrs Molleson: "Dr Desmond not being at home she was placed in a cab and sent to the infirmary. Her parents were immediately informed and have been to see her." Sadly Caroline died the next day from shock. An inquest recorded a verdict of "Accidental Death" and the Reverend Sydney Turner, the Government Inspector, recommended that a tap be affixed to the boiler.

The floor of the laundry was constantly awash and there were many instances of girls and staff slipping and breaking limbs. Harsh soap peeled the skin off chilblained hands and the dank, foul atmosphere and searing fumes took toll on constitutionally

Delinquent girls could expect stern treatment but the laundry girls worked the hardest, often in appalling conditions. (School for delinquent girls, Ford, Liverpool)

weakened lungs and rheumaticky limbs. Complexions were toasted and withered from the heat of the ironing stove on which the large, heavy and cumbersome irons lined up for duty. The suffering of the girls was so acute that in 1897 a screen was erected to protect them from the fierce blast of the stove.

Fashionable women of the day wore endless petticoats, under-skirts, over-skirts, tucks, flounces and trimmings. Ironing required meticulous care and a high standard of perfection was demanded by the ladies who sent in their finery to the reformatory school laundry. There were several instances of customers withdrawing their custom through dissatisfaction and these usually involved the subsequent dismissal of the laundress.

In the drying room, two fires were kept going in an attempt to dry out the clothes after they had been laboriously mangled several times. In 1899, the economy-minded Committee rebuked the laundress for using excessive quantities of coke for this purpose, but in the end they had no choice but to replace the succession of thoroughly worn-out mangles with new ones. The situation was eased a little in 1898 with the arrival of a centrifugal wringing-machine at a cost of £21.

The dirty washing arrived in giant skips. As well as the laundry from private families, nursing homes and the occasional hotel, the school washed for the 150 boys on board the training ship Conway. The charge was 1/- per dozen articles, reduced by the penny-pinching Conway committee to 11d a dozen, and hammocks at 4d each. Repairs were also handled, the rate charged being 2/6d per boy for each term.

Ever present was the risk of infection. At the height of an influenza epidemic in May 1901 Dr Nevin, the Medical Officer, recommended that all the pocket handkerchiefs sent to the school should be transported in a separate hamper and immediately placed in a boiler and disinfected in that way. During the outbreaks of measles, diphtheria and scarlet fever on board the Conway, the boys' clothing was disinfected under the direction of the ship's MO.

The income from this industry was a highly valued asset for the Liverpool Reformatory Committee. It ranged from £20 19s 8d to £48 7s 2d per fortnight. This high figure was as a result of a special washing job for the North Western Hotel, and the two laundry matrons were each given a £22 gratuity and the girls a day out at New Brighton in consideration for the extra work. In 1894 the total amount received for washing was £493 16s 6d.

Until 1899, when the collection and deliveries were taken over by a carrier firm with a horse and cart, the girls were deliberately placed in positions of trust to collect and deliver the linen of private families. They were responsible for the collecting of the laundry bill monies, and their behaviour and honesty was a test of how deserving they were of the confidence placed in them and their eventual recommendation for a job in service. Matron Mrs Molleson was only occasionally disappointed, the main offenders being the girls unable to resist their sweet tooth, who, depositing their skips outside the door, nipped into sweetshops en route and helped themselves to toffee. For this offence they were severely punished.

On the whole the girls worked hard and cheerfully, several taking advantage of the system to set up their own laundries in later years; no doubt others were inspired to continue their toil by the words of HM Inspector, the Reverend Sydney Turner: "I am glad to find that so many of you girls make good and useful wives," and "idle hands need work, and continuous industry produces the happiest results in your character." The occasional girl who did rebel like Margretha, who confessed to smashing the gas pipes in the laundry, was placed in solitary confinement for three days on a diet of bread and water. It was not surprising that in October 1901 the Liverpool Reformatory Association subscribed £1 1s to the laundry committee of the Reformatory and Refuge Union, towards the expenses of opposing a proposal to bring laundries of charitable institutions under the Factory Act.

Other Activities

Presuming that the girls had some energy left over for recreational pursuits, the programme of activities planned for them more or less guaranteed the elimination of every ounce of surplus zest and wickedness of intention.

Observed one Inspector in 1898: "There can be no question that a vigorous course of physical culture will do these girls lasting good, moral as well as physical."
"Gymnastics cannot be taught to the same extent among girls as boys but musical drill is the nearest approach. I was delighted to observe the dumb bells being used as vigorously as ever, with the girls taking much pleasure. Their vigour is a refreshing spectacle."

And in 1903: "There was a fair display of physical drill. I should like to see the drill in the girls' school up to the level of that in the boys' school. Upright carriage and a graceful manner of walking are valuable assets to a girl going out to service, and the regular practice which helps to secure them is a most healthy exercise. A good deal more time should be devoted to it."

So drill with free exercise and movements with bar bells were carried on daily for all but the laundry girls, who practised once a week. Some of the girls developed muscles comparable with Irish navvies, and the vigorous twirling of the dumb bells expanded their busts. Brassieres, referred to cryptically in a committee report as "an innovation regarding certain articles of underwear", were purchased for the girls in 1915.

In their cumbersome calico skirts and high-necked, long-sleeved blouses, the girls were put through their drill paces by a Mrs Herbert Campbell, who had a voice that would have done justice to any parade ground, and the keen eye of a sergeant major seeking perfection.

They went walking for two hours every Saturday, more frequently when the ladies of the Visiting Committee could spare the time to escort them in small parties, but the best part of the day for the girls not already exhausted was one hour for play in the garden every day. This pleasurable pastime was carried out at the double with fairly hectic games of ball and hop-scotch and sitting around firmly discouraged. Girls who were not strong were given more exercise to toughen them up. There were swings at the bottom of the garden and the girls lined up obediently for a brief ecstatic exploration into the magical world of a childhood which had so far eluded them. For the little ones, some as young as 11, there was the handing of a much-coveted doll and carriage. For many of the children this was the first doll they had ever handled, and over the years the soulless little china face with the vacant blue eyes, which had previously kept illustrious company in the nursery of a rich merchant, was their special friend to receive secret messages and the caress of small eager hands, to compensate in a few minutes for all the grimness of their hours of reality. Some of the older girls had small flower pots, and there was a library of carefully vetted books and magazines with story-lines upholding the excellence of goodness.

All the girls were taught to make their own clothing and knitted their stockings. Sewing class at Ford

Every girl went through a course of twenty cookery lessons, until the First World War when a shortage of ingredients made it impossible to continue and they were encouraged to keep notes of recipes and useful hints. Proficient in every aspect of housewifery, they made excellent servants and in 1903 the demand exceeded the supply. The Committee noted: "There is no difficulty in finding employment for our girls, as they are much sought after as servants. Some of them are getting £12 a year in their first place and six girls in service have money deposited in the Post Office Savings Bank." In 1902, the Committee had ordered that earnings hitherto paid to girls in service should be paid to the Superintendent, she allowing small necessary amounts to the girls and the balance booked to the credit of the Superintendent at the Savings Bank for providing the girls with clothing at her discretion.

In spite of the length and hard toil of their working hours, many of the girls remained in the same situation for long periods, one girl staying with the same mistress for 27 years. Latterly the reward money for remaining in the same situation for three years was replaced with a prize of a silver watch and chain.

It was quite exceptional for a girl to be sent back from service for misconduct. If one returned at all, it was usually due to ill health. For example, Ada limped in with a housemaid's knee and May had broken her ankle. Their places were filled temporarily with a fit girl until the invalids had recovered sufficiently to return to duty.

The aim of the religious teachings which claimed a large part of the school curriculum was to provide a central moral basis on which could be developed a sense of responsibility towards themselves and others. Time was set aside each day for scripture and bible readings, prayers and hymns, with religious instruction from the school chaplain on Monday, Thursday and Friday. The duties of the chaplain appointed in 1897 at a salary of £40 per annum were stated to be: "General superintendence of religious instruction; visitation of the sick when in hospital; superintendence of confirmation classes on Tuesday evenings. Take general interest in religious concerns of the school and that the girls have religious teaching or service at the school on Sunday evening to avoid the inconvenience of walking to and from the church through the streets."

The girls were regularly examined by the Diocesan Inspector, who reported: "October 19th 1892. The general appearance and excellent order of the girls speak as plainly of the unremitting care for their bodily welfare, as the intelligent and reverent answers given in the examination do of constant and careful spiritual instruction. I use the word spiritual in preference to religious, because I find in each of the groups far more attempted and accomplished than often comes under the name of religious instruction. Every part of the scripture studied is made to yield its spiritual lesson; the catechism is treated not merely as a form of sound words, but in direct relation to life.

"I am pleased to be able to report a continuance of earnest and practical religious teaching, a healthy and high tone among the inmates, and much intelligence in their reception of religious instruction, as shewn by their answers to questions upon Old and New Testament history, and on the meaning and application of the church catechism. The method of instruction pursued with regard to the latter has been eminently practical; in all groups I found the girls able to supply what might otherwise be dry formulae to the facts they had learnt in the scriptures, and vice versa to draw from the scripture lessons, proofs and illustrations of the catechism. Naturally the answers given by the elder girls are more thoughtful than those of younger groups, but in none is there any of the guessing at a reply which sometimes does duty for knowledge, nor any appearance of mechanical memory as distinguished from intelligent appreciation."

"Moreover, as far as I am judge, the consciences of the girls have been awakened to the spiritual importance of the lessons given. I must speak highly of the care shown in the written work, and of the reverent tone of the singing and repetition.

"The memories of the children are being stored with truths which are of the highest importance to be felt and retained. The effect of this must be to help in moulding their character and lives, and to elevate them in a way impossible without it. That this is attained in many instances is manifest from what is known of considerable numbers whose course of life has been followed and enquired into."

Rewards

The perks for dutiful behaviour were well worthwhile. There was a silver watch for the year's most obedient girl and four work-boxes for the most industrious. Girls from "law-abiding" homes were allowed to visit every six weeks as a reward for behaving themselves.

Good girls visited the Walker Art Gallery to view the paintings and were allowed to take advantage of, for example, the offer of a free visit to Manders' Menagerie and a request from school mistress Miss Dixon to allow selected girls to attend church on her wedding day. Local residents also invited some for "a splendid bread and butter tea and bunloaf." At the New Ferry home of a rich shipowner, tea was enjoyed to music by the bandboys from the Akbar, and a concert was given by Miss Pearson, the singing teacher, who was described as being in "fine voice". Particularly worth striving for was a day out at New Brighton, travelling free one way on the ferry across the Mersey by courtesy of the ferry manager and with special permission from Matron to wear Sunday dresses for the occasion.

In 1881, girls who were worthy of the treat were taken to see Queen Victoria on her visit to Liverpool and provided with buns and oranges. Many of them were in tears as they waved their paper Union Jacks from a special vantage point, while the Queen passed by in a carriage pulled by a magnificent team of horses.

There was strong emphasis in all the Liverpool Reformatory Association schools on loyalty to Queen and Country, and special dates of celebration, such as the Queen's Birthday, were made more memorable for the girls by gifts, usually oranges and a box of prunes. Each of the 520 children at the three schools was given a Coronation Cup purchased from the Doulton Pottery Works in celebration of the King's Coronation in May 1902.

There were times when, no matter how deserving their behaviour or how patriotic the occasion, the children were refused permission by the Committee to attend. In 1903 an invitation from the Lord Mayor of Liverpool for the Reformatory girls to take part in the King's Birthday festivities was turned down on the grounds that they would have to be under surveillance and mix with children from other schools. As far as the Committee were concerned, they were not good enough.

Sewing, embroidery and knitting kept fingers busy and eyesight strained during the dark winter evenings. Friends of the Committee provided welcome diversions such as limelight lectures, concerts, magic lantern and wax works, and there was a welcome gift of a worn harmonium.

At Christmas, the spirit of goodwill towards all girls affected the whole of the Association and behaviour improved dramatically. It began a few days before Christmas with an escorted walk in small groups around the Liverpool shops to gaze in the decorated windows at the displays of toys, pretty dresses, shawls and bonnets, presents, sweets and bon-bons. Abundant gifts of holly and evergreens arrived to decorate the spartan rooms, and there was a large Christmas tree which the girls decked with candles and coloured paper streamers. Enthused Matron Miss Laurie in her report in 1897: "The faces of the girls reflected pink and rosy their happiness in the glow of the firelight. They clapped their hands in delight and their eyes widened in gleeful anticipation as they viewed the fine Christmas tree loaded with useful presents." There was a picture, a book, an orange, some nuts, muscatels and a pair of hand-knitted cuffs, donated by well-wishers, for each girl. Also a letter for each girl and officer from the Christmas Letter Society. Of all the pleasures of that day there was none to equal the never-to-be-forgotten turkeys provided for Christmas dinner. "After dinner they sang carols and played games and at the end of the day they knelt down in prayer to thank the Heavenly father for the best Christmas they had ever had."

The luxury most greatly anticipated apart from Christmas came in the latter years, a 14-day camp at Heswall on the Wirral. Old girls who could manage to arrange their holidays at the same time were invited to join. Wrote Matron Miss Maxwell in 1906: "I cannot say enough to express my appreciation of the 'Holiday

Home' beautifully situated on the River Dee. The girls and staff migrated there on August 12th for a fortnight. There the girls are seen in their true characters. A desire for higher and better life is showing itself among them, and is a redeeming feature even in some whose conduct did not until now encourage much hope for their improvement. Opening intelligence was shown in the collections made in their rambles, and in their thirst for knowledge of the various features of nature around them. We walked and studied elementary botany and collected interesting leaves and flowers to be pressed and preserved in books. All returned home greatly benefitted both physically and morally. The holiday was greatly enjoyed and the 'bramble bushes' are the only sufferers from our visit."

An earlier camp at Hightown near Liverpool was more spartan. Sixty girls attended in August 1900, when the London & North Western Railway Company charged each adult 10d and the children travelled at half fare. The Committee paid £6 6s a week for the use of the camp house, including water and 3 cwt of coal, and an additional 2/6d for the use of each tent. The girls took their own bedding.

Among Friends of the Committee, the goodwill continued throughout the year with gifts of firewood, lettuce, kidney-beans, jars of jam, rhubarb, flower seeds for their gardening plots, barrels of apples, tartlets and bunloaves on special occasions, sweets to be handed out for good conduct, and eggs, grapes and cake for those in the sick room.

Other excitements included visits by important local ladies in fine clothes who embellished many a school occasion, like a Mrs Legge who "so gracefully declared the new dining hall open."

Drink and Disease

Under the banner of temperance the evil of drunkenness was driven home in all of the reformatory schools by committees determined to save the lads and girls from the curse and slavery of drink, and to convince their young charges that sobriety was the only safe and worthwhile path. Those in authority regarded drink just as apprehensively as we do drug-taking and glue-sniffing among the young today. For the masses it was an escape route from the hardship and problems of reality. In the oblivion of alcohol they found a brief solace of sorts but, to the reformers, alcohol was an evil power and the material factor in the downfall of both men and women, weakening moral fibre and creating criminals. Temperance society speakers with a strong message on the subject, and latterly with jars of pickled livers to illustrate its ravages, were warmly welcomed to address the boys and girls, who wrote essays on the subject to make sure the message had been absorbed.

Staff who were seen in school in a state of intoxication were frequently dismissed. The Committee listened in horror to Matron's report on Miss Riley, who returned to school with "hat askew, her eyes glazed and smelling strongly of gin." In 1864 Rosie, who was returned from her situation as an upstairs maid for "getting tipsy but otherwise of an excellent character," had her licence revoked. A girl brought back to school by her father in March 1871, because she and her mother had been out drinking together, was promptly re-admitted. Margaret, a free (uncommitted) case whose father offered 2/- a week for her board, was taken in after it was noted with some concern that the family lived next door to the Phoenix Inn in Kirkdale. In November 1900 a letter from Dr Nevins, the Medical Officer, asking that a supply of beer be allowed for the sewing mistress for medicinal purposes, was unanimously refused.

The position of Medical Officer to a reformatory school was onerous and the recompense poor, considering the amount of work and time involved. In 1902 Dr Warburton was appointed MO of the girls' school, to be paid £30 per annum in lieu of fees.

The sick room was a spartan affair with iron bedsteads, a wash stand, looking glass, chair and linoleum-covered floor. The older girls performed the nursing duties in a "very satisfactory manner," under the direction of the Medical Officer, and there were several instances of devotion to duty and tender care being rewarded with a present of 10/-. Some of the girls who showed outstanding nursing skills were recommended by the doctor to hospitals, as trainee nurses. One such girl finished up a matron.

Sickness was an ever-present problem for the reformers. Death was a frequent visitor as children and adults succumbed to explosive epidemics of diphtheria, scarlatina, typhus, smallpox, tuberculosis, chicken-pox and measles. The constitutionally weak girls were easy prey to every infection accidentally introduced to the school, and classroom numbers were decimated at varying intervals. In 1907 there were 52 girls in hospital with diphtheria and an epidemic of mumps resulting from the admittance of a sick girl from Holloway. Influenza took its toll in 1918 on 58 girls, 28 of whom were sent to hospital seriously ill, and there were four deaths. Girls with smallpox were sent to the isolation hospital and the remaining girls were vaccinated, with the Committee postponing its regular meeting at the school until the infection had cleared. Consumptive girls with no family or friends were sent to the workhouse to die. Outbreaks of diarrhoea were commonplace. After 60 girls were taken ill in 1910, drainage work was carried out at a cost of £20. Ringworm, eczema and impetigo spread rapidly. A case of ringworm brought in on a smuggled letter resulted in 20 cases "rapidly spreading" in 1914. The Medical Officer advised hospital treatment with X-ray at a cost of £12. No discharges or admissions were allowed until the infection had cleared. In the early days, an inadequate water supply and defective drainage resulted in a constant fear of an outbreak of typhus fever. Indeed, there was a case of typhus in the school as recently as 1920, the year 21 girls were despatched to hospital with scarlatina.

A number of girls died, some from rapid consumption like 12-year-old May in 1875. The Matron reported: "Her deathbed was most happy, as far as we are able to judge, and her advice and counsel to others were most touching. We have had three cases of serious illness this year." Parents were encouraged to be with a dying child. In 1906, referring to Mary who became ill nine days before Christmas with pleurisy and pneumonia, the Matron declared: "It was gratifying that the mother of the girl had time to travel from London and arrive in time to see her child before she died. The woman expressed great thankfulness to the authorities for their goodness to her daughter." The mother, who was unable to read or write, dictated the following letter to a "letter writer", to be forwarded to the school Matron. "Mrs Brown is anxious I should write to you to express all her gratitude for your kindly care of her daughter Mary, and for your kindness to her and to her husband. She feels very deeply all your kindness to her, and your kindness and interest in Mary. It is quite beautiful to hear of such a peaceful deathbed, and she must have been well looked after, and well trained to face death in the fearless way she did."

The Matron's report went on: "The mother, who is a good woman, quite sees all is for the best, and quite realises that Mary's Christmas will be much happier than her own."

Epileptic girls were discharged to the workhouse. Nonsense girls like Sarah, who "feigned going out of her mind," usually responded to a sound ticking-off by making a swift recovery. A fair number of girls had suicidal tendencies but attempts to end their lives rarely succeeded and in this present age would have been recognised for what they were, cries for attention and help.

To the reformers, serious suicide attempts were acts of madness. Girls like Lena, who tried to strangle herself; Sabrina, who would have managed to hang herself had she found a stronger piece of string; Mary, who cut her throat and Ann, who admitted taking laudanum because she did not like her post as a parlour maid, were discharged to mental asylums. Others were given a second chance.

HM Inspector referred to one of them as "very peculiar who alarmed the school by an apparent attempt at suicide. She did not hurt herself much and for some months has been behaving satisfactorily," he said. Another girl, Jenny, who was committed to the school on a charge of attempted suicide and who upon arrival seemed to be completely "abandoned to the mania", decided with firm handling that life was worthwhile after all and rose to become a schoolroom monitress and a graduate to the 7th standard.

Some of the girls had sad physical defects, which in the ordinary run of their hapless lives would surely have been neglected. There were several examples of special help and extra care for these unfortunates in the minutes of the association over the years. Ellen was sent to hospital in 1912 for the removal of a squint which made her the object of many hurtful jests by her companions and earned her the nickname of "cock-eyed Ellen". A spinal support was obtained for Agnes, and a trained nurse to care for Ada, very ill with pneumonia. A concerned eye was kept on Margaret, who remained in hospital nearly a whole year with psoriasis, and Nelly, a phthisical case who was in hospital for four months.

Esther, a girl out on licence, was allowed to stay at the school for a fortnight in 1904, so that the Medical Officer could treat her nose and throat daily at his home. Ada was sent for seven weeks' convalescence at a home at West Kirby to help her recuperate from pneumonia. From Jessie in 1909, "the dentist having drawn all her teeth, it was decided to supply her with false teeth." She was one of several girls who was given dentures.

Deaf and dumb Annie was sent in 1900 to a special school as a day scholar for 2/- per quarter. She was reported later to be making good progress and "much brighter looking than when she arrived." In 1904, Eliza, with a severe eye complaint, was sent to hospital for her third operation after a matron had reported: "Her sight does not allow her to do either school, sewing or laundry work." Lilly, of indifferent health, had an operation for an enlarged gland. No-one could help Emily, who in 1905 was reported as being mentally and physically unfit for industrial training. She was sent to the workhouse.

Special arrangements were made in 1905 for the Bishop of Liverpool to hold a private confirmation service in the sickroom for Victoria, too ill to attend the service in church. Many of her young companions squeezed into the room to watch and the Matron reported: "This was a most touching service and the words spoken by the kind Bishop must remain with these young people for the rest of their lives."

In Loco Parentis

The Reformatory Association demanded total obedience and trustworthiness, and their parental rod of censure was swift to crack down at the slightest suggestion of breach of discipline. Nevertheless, their role as surrogate parent did not lack genuine concern. They acted as legal watchdog for Leah of Toxteth. Hearing that her bank book containing £16 and her father's watch were in the hands of an unscrupulous relative, they instructed a solicitor to get them back.

Fanny, a destitute case from Yorkshire whose time at the school had expired, was allowed to remain for an extra month in the hope that she would be found a job in service. Another girl with a "wretched" home was permitted to stay until a situation was found for her as well.

When they heard that the mother of May could not afford to visit her daughter, not expected to recover from tubercular meningitis in hospital, they paid the mother's expenses. In 1915 the mother of Edith, a girl with phthisis, asked that her daughter should return home and the Committee did their best to persuade the mother to leave the girl in hospital because of the possibility of infection to the other children in the family.

In 1899, two guineas was spent on a weighing machine with the order that all girls should be regularly weighed and measured. It became routine for each of them on arrival to be examined by the doctor, who carefully checked on teeth, eyes, ears and tonsils.

With the astuteness of a thrifty housewife, no effort was spared over the years to shop around for supplies of good quality which could be bought cheaply. Under the watchful eye of HM Inspector, the diet improved over the years, with more consideration given to a correct and healthy balance and more variety than the previous monotonous fare of porridge, bread and treacle, and beast's head broth with vegetables.

In April 1899 a bread and butter tea replaced porridge on Saturdays. In 1904 each girl's milk allowance was raised to half a pint each day. The official order of 1915 that each be given 8 ounces of bread at meal times irritated the Committee, who were paying 50/- per 100 loaves and anxious to avoid waste, they decided that 6 ounces would suffice, with more for those who asked for it.

The First World War years were very trying. The girls lost weight owing to the reduction in meat and magarine, and in spite of extra rations of potatoes, peas and herring. Cookery classes were disbanded owing to difficulty in obtaining meat. To satisfy the appetites of hungry, growing young girls was a constant battle and ingenious recipes were tried to give the homely potato a more inviting image. A high incidence of tuberculosis ravaged the school in January 1916, bringing a letter from the Home Office directing that the number of inmates be reduced from 90 to 70. Bitter weather the following November brought many colds, bronchial complaints and general debility and resulted in the girls being regularly dosed with cod liver oil and Fellows Syrup.

Troubles at Toxteth

Some of the most troublesome girls were at the Toxteth School. In March 1897, the Toxteth Park Girls' Reformatory at 9 Parkhill Road, its buildings, furniture, fittings and monies totalling £318 18s 9d, with the responsibilities of its management but free from debt of any kind, was offered to the Liverpool Reformatory Association. For the previous 42 years the school had been managed by a committee of local benefactors, presided over by a Mrs Herbert Campbell from a fashionable and leading family.

The success of the Liverpool Reformatory Association in its handling of young male and female offenders had earned it a nationwide reputation, and the Committee's advice was often sought by similar bodies throughout the country. Toxteth Park Girls' Reformatory was one of two schools - the other being Edge Hill - which merged with the Association, thereby increasing the total number of boys and girls within the group to 500 at the end of the nineteenth century.

The saga of the Toxteth Park Reformatory was not new to the Liverpool Reformatory Association. In 1860, when rowdy trouble-makers had threatened to disrupt the day-to-day running of the school, the toughest matron in the Liverpool Association was brought in on loan. She was a Miss Molleson, a most successful matron who remained with the Association for many years. After just one month of her presence at Toxteth, peace returned and the Committee reported that "she was very successful in her efforts at bringing the girls under control." Miss Molleson's salary was £80 a year and 9/- a week board.

Her reign coincided with one of the toughest periods of crackdown on young offenders with no nonsense tolerated by the schools or courts. Typical of the punishments doled out was what happened to Ann, a pretty, obstreperous bundle of mischief, who absconded while cleaning the front step and was brought back by a policeman a few hours later. She was sent to prison for three months and returned from Walton Gaol "much subdued". Another absconder, Jane, was not sufficiently contrite when she appeared before Mr Raffles, the Stipendiary Magistrate. He told her: "You are so very saucy, I am sending you to prison for three months."

As was to be expected the change of management at Toxteth created restlessness among the girls, with frequent absconding and additional trouble arising from quickness or obstinacy of temper, violence, disobedience and insolence, and the serious offences of lying, theft and immorality. In the first year there were 43 misdemeanours recorded, the worst being three cases of pilfering, with a high incidence of nipping to freedom over the garden wall or disappearing from church, and much general insubordination. Punishment included loss of marks, corporal punishment or restriction in the padded cell.

At the turn of the century the cost of maintenance and instruction for a nine month period worked out at £14 13s 6d per head on an average of 59 girls, with an industrial profit of £113 5s 2d.

Reported Government Inspector James Legge: "Owing to the numerous changes in staff and the unsettled state of the girls, I found the conduct and discipline very unsatisfactory. There was a good bit of insubordination, laziness and insolence to be put down.
"The school room has been a weak point during the year, both as regards instruction and discipline, and it is to be hoped there will be an improvement during the coming year. A new teacher, with experience in dealing with industrial school children, is needed."

The history of the Toxteth School in particular was patterned with disturbances, some more serious than others. Compared with the riotous behaviour of today, the youthful disorder of yester-year was usually more defiant than destructive, but to those in authority, unwilling to tolerate any challenge to their control, it was shocking in the extreme.

On November 7th 1901 the Committee were deeply troubled when Matron Miss Crane reported that a serious disturbance had taken place. It had happened on the night of Wednesday, October 30th, shortly after she had returned from holiday.

She said, "The girls did not receive me with their usual welcome, and did not say 'Good Night', as was usual when I left them after prayers. The following day there was a considerable amount of disobedience and insulting manner to myself and to Miss Marsh, the new Assistant Matron.

"I asked the reason for such misconduct and they said they had been kept short of food during my absence and that some of the food had been badly cooked. There was also a remark by some of them that I had been very cross to them before I left on holiday. Captain Price came to speak to the girls on the subject of their misconduct who by holding up their hands expressed their sorrow for what they had done and promised not to repeat it."

An investigation into the complaints resulted in the Assistant Matron being dismissed for spoiling the girls' and officers' food, and the resignation of Miss Crane, who refused to accede to a suggestion that she take half a day off a week instead of a whole day, to exercise greater control.

A riot which occurred at 1.30pm on March 12th 1912 proved a disaster for Matron Miss Struthers, who had arrived to take up her duties only on the previous evening. She was young, attractive and a little apprehensive, not having as yet established her authority. The Toxteth girls recognised the situation at a glance, and decided that the opportunity to challenge her control was too good to be missed.

A dejected Miss Struthers reported: "I entered on my duties here on the evening of the 18th. Next day at 1.30pm 18 girls refused to pay any attention to the bell summoning them to work, and remained in the yard dancing and singing. After the Assistant went for them they came to the workroom and then 10 only started to work, the remaining 8 refused to obey any orders. They disturbed the house and neighbourhood by dancing, singing, and marching around the room, jumping on the forms and continued to do so for four hours. At 6 o'clock, Mr Jones arrived and they were asked to apologise. All did but one girl named May who refused absolutely and a constable was called in. While she was being allowed time to consider, some fighting ensued among the girls who had apologised, and a hysterical girl outside of the workroom broke a window. For twenty minutes the scene was one of a riot; finally May was taken to Essex Street Bridewell."

Such a situation was seen to reflect the weakness of those in control and, after interviews, frequently led to the resignation of the person supposedly in authority. This was so in the case of Miss Struthers, who tendered her resignation, admitting that she was unable to maintain school discipline. The Committee resolved that she be paid £7 10s.

Staff who lost patience and took the punishment into their own hands - like a Miss Parkinson who in 1898 "boxed a girl's ears" - were severely reprimanded and usually resigned, having lost face with the girls and forfeited the faith of the controllers. Miss Parkinson was no exception.

The Toxteth girls were on the whole taller than the others. Inspector Legge reported in 1897: "The girls seem unusually tall for this class of girls, but some of them should be taught to hold themselves better." But whatever they lacked in deportment and righteousness, they gave of their best in other spheres. In 1908 specimens of needlework, essays, cookery and photographs of them in service were sent to the Franco-British Exhibition in London. They won cups for needlework, recitation and obtained national honours for needlework in a competition at St George's Hall in 1919. Two years later, competing in the inter-schools' contest, they brought back two silver cups, one for swimming and the other for singing. Their success reflected great credit on the reformatory school Committee.

Relaxing the Rules

There were strict rules for girls out on licence. None could be sent on licence until she had been in the school two and a half years, unless under exceptional circumstances which had to be approved. In all cases, a monthly conduct report had to be made by all employers, and, in any case of a girl leaving, notice of intention was required to be sent in good time by her employer and she had to return to the reformatory.

Some prospective employers were wary about accepting the responsibility for girls on licence. June and Ann were sent back from a factory because they were giving so much trouble. The manager was worried that if they ran away, he might be answerable for their bad behaviour.

A parents' petition to the Home Secretary in 1900 for their daughter to be licensed was refused, when the Matron objected on account of her indolent and unsatisfactory behaviour at school. The girls in service in town were visited regularly by the matron. Cases of absconding from their situation and of serious misconduct were reported to her immediately.

The staff in the early days were severely hampered by lack of communication with the outside world. In an emergency it was left to Matron's enterprise to try to cool down an explosive situation until she had confirmed appropriate punishment for the offenders. Occasionally the delaying factor worked in favour of the culprit. On April 2nd 1860 a telegram from Newcastle Police informed the matron that a girl escapee had been taken into custody. Miss Cuthbert wrote by return of post requesting that she be detained, but by the time the letter arrived, she had been set at liberty. The situation was greatly improved in February 1898, when a private telephone line connecting each school to the Committee office was installed at a cost of £22 10s a year.

Honesty was very much insisted upon by the Liverpool reformers and a girl was seldom punished if she spoke the truth. Moral strength was often put to the test. For example Ellen, who picked a pocket while out on an errand, was allowed to go out again after her punishment, to be trusted under proper supervision.

It was a hard struggle to make good champion over the evil-doer and the Committee began and ended each meeting with a prayer for spiritual help and guidance. The heavenly inspiration of the Good Lord was greatly assisted by the practical nature of the firm punishments permitted in the early days of the reformatory association.

At the dawn of the twentieth century the era of toughness was on the wane. Cropping girls' hair, one of the most effective forms of punishment, had been phased out after a Home Office Inspector protested: "I greatly dislike the punishment of hair cutting and think it should only be resorted to in really extreme cases such as violent insubordination or indecency."

"It should certainly be confined to the younger girls and never done at the order only of the superintendent. Like all penalties that appeal more directly to personal pride and self-respect it acts very unequally, some girls caring much, others nothing at all, about it. I shall be glad to see it practically erased from the list of punishments."

By 1910 the wind of change was blowing gustily, forcing away the old rules and beginning to make the juvenile offender's life easier. It had officially breezed in with a gentle puff in 1907, when the Inspector suggested mildly that to make life less hard, girls should be provided with brushes with long handles to make floor polishing easier and to replace the old style method of crawling along the floor, shining the wood or linoleum with a heavy cloth, polish and plenty of elbow grease. Next to be abolished were the standard three days in the dark eeriness of a cold cell, which had proved a frightening and chastening experience for many a naughty girl, and the padded cell. Obviously not convinced of their deterrent value, the Inspector noted: "their very existence must have a demoralising effect on the school."

The Home Office, working through its Chief Inspector, had held considerable powers over the running of the reformatory schools since the inception of the Youthful Offenders' Act of 1854. There were a number of confrontations over the years between the Home Office and the Liverpool Reformatory Committee, the latter resenting the interference of HM Inspector and questioning his judgement.

The Inspector always won in the end and his control was unquestionable as the years progressed. In 1911, the then Mr Winston Churchill set up a committee to inquire in general into the constitutions, management, discipline and education of Reformatory and Industrial Schools in England and Wales, the qualifications of staff, remuneration, and the suitability of ships for use as schools. They also considered very carefully the superintendence of boys and girls after leaving the schools. The findings of that committee led to many changes ... and the Home Office directives came in thick and fast.

In 1915 the order went out to destroy the birch by burning, as "it must in no case be used in punishing the girls" and it was suggested, "when necessary a light school cane or tawse should be used." Superintendents had to furnish a list of all forms of punishment to an Inspector. The old school uniforms were to be replaced, with brighter shades of material for dresses and coats instead of cloaks. Night commodes were abolished and the locking of dormitory doors was to be discontinued. Home leave was to be permitted and the girls were allowed to talk at meals. More frequent opportunities for letter writing must be given. New school room desks and better lighting were to be provided and the staff were to take their meals with the girls.

There were those among the Committee who shook their heads in protest, gloomily predicting that phasing out many of their most effective forms of punishment and weakening the rules would allow standards of discipline to slip and produce a whiplash of disorder.

It was perhaps the turning point in the history of the old-style reformatories when the benefactors, who had tried to run things their way for sixty years, were finally forced to accept a lesser authority and capitulate to the Home Office and its own particular form of rule.

The Committee's last stand was in February 1912, with a demand for clarification on the whole question of corporal punishment and a refusal to admit "refractory girls" until it was permitted. HM Inspector Robertson was requested to consult the Home Secretary. Meanwhile girls of bad conduct were taken before the magistrate and sentenced to Borstal for three years. The official explanation was clear and firm. With the burning of the birch rod, only the swish of the cane was left as punishment. Even that could be used only when absolutely necessary.

The last few years

In later years, apprehension as to overstepping the mark with punishment led to a natural reluctance to take any such steps without first consulting an Inspector. Concern over what was acceptable spread to the Medical Officer, who enquired about his right to forcible feeding in the case of necessity. The Home Office laid down that this would be justified in order to prevent death or serious injury to health.

The easing of rigid standards, one by one, brought anxiety to those in control of young lives. In 1912 there were three resignations at Toxteth, including the superintendent, deputy superintendent and sewing mistress. Four years later, four of the staff were off ill, two "broken down in health". Deprived of the old rules, they were frequently frustrated in their efforts to quell the usual list of offences such as impudence, absconding, theft, bad language, violent conduct and refusal to work. They tried the new system of deprivation of marks and privileges, and more troublemakers were passed on to the courts for periods of Borstal and probation.

In 1920 with special permission five girls received corporal punishment for stealing £3 from the sewing matron's bedroom. They were the last girls to be caned at the home before it closed in 1921.

The new Governmental watchdog system also looked more carefully into the health of the children and in particular at the worrying epidemic of tuberculosis which was taking its toll. Dr Ada, attending at Toxteth in 1915, examined 66 girls and stressed the necessity for supplying them with slippers and a separate mug for each girl when cleaning her teeth. It was a sensible precaution against the raging tuberculosis infection. Four of the girls were in Toxteth Infirmary on the day of her visit: Violet, Vera and Annie with tubercular glands, Margaret with mumps. Emily, suffering from anaemia, a weak heart and poor circulation, was ill in school, as was Fanny, prostrate with a gastric disturbance and showing signs of commencing consumption.

The last few months of the girls' school were far from happy. The conduct of the girls was most unsatisfactory and there were further resignations of staff unable to cope. The laundry work had almost finished and the current earnings from that source were consequently reduced to 18/7d. There was a desperate need for work to keep the girls occupied and out of mischief. The matron reported "the absolute necessity of more work being done by the girls for their health and general well-being," and "I have decided to take in some further private family washing." The pendulum had swung the other way.

Additional problems for the Committee were rising costs and the inability to keep staff, the result of constant pressure from the Home Office to tighten up on wages and make general economies. Outside fund raising and donations had fallen off. An attempt to revive social balls on modified lines in the season 1919/20 failed. Could it be that the only workable scheme would be to restore a first class ball and supper, with good music on pre-war lines?

It was something of a relief when on October 24th 1921, a letter came from the Home Secretary seeking the withdrawal of the girls' school licence.

On December 12th 1921, there were 40 girls left at Toxteth, three in hospital and eighteen on licence. Three of the staff remaining packed their carpet bags and, having found other situations, left on the 31st. It was decided that 14 girls would be licensed to situations and the remainder transferred to other reformatories.

The valuation of the property exclusive of furniture amounted to £4,370 and a decision was taken to sell at £5,000. The furniture brought £284 15s 1d. Today, number 9 Parkhill Road, situated on the fringe of Liverpool 8, has disappeared under the bulldozer.

No-one can dispute that managing the reformatory girls within the Liverpool Association was anything but a formidable labour fraught with circumstances which tried the forbearance of the most heavenly-minded. Nevertheless, throughout 66 years dealing with young girl delinquents, the Liverpool Committee achieved an impressive measure of success.

Between 1855 and 1906 a total of 877 girls was admitted to Toxteth Park School. Of these: 21 died, 15 were transferred, 456 sent to service and 239 to friends, 6 emigrated, 18 absconded and were sentenced, 3 sent to prison, 30 were discharged on account of disease and 20 by special warrant. The total discharged was 808, with 69 under detention on December 31st 1906.

During the 49 years existence of Mount Vernon Green between the years 1857 and 1906, the total number received amounted to 1,213. Of these: 22 died, 9 were transferred, 1 sent to an asylum, 638 to service, 357 to friends, 13 emigrated, 28 absconded, 7 went to prison, 43 were discharged on account of disease and 12 by special warrant. The total discharged was 1,130, with 84 under detention on December 31st 1906.

Miss Maxwell, matron in 1906, wrote words which could be an accolade for all the staff: "When I see the girls leaving the Home with new desires and firm determination to live a different life, I feel my work has not been in vain." Many old girls who held their heads up high and strolled the fashionable suburbs would have agreed with her.

FARM SCHOOL
Preparing the Ground

October 2nd 1858: *"Liverpool Juvenile Reformatory Association, Hackins Hey, Liverpool.*
Wanted for a Market Garden, 30 to 80 acres of land, with a good house and farm buildings, either in Lancashire or Cheshire, and within about 15 miles of Liverpool, on a lease of not less than 7 years.

Apply by letter, to John Cropper, Esq, Honorary Secretary."

John Cropper could never have supposed it possible that, 128 years later, the third arm of the Association's plan to help children in trouble would have developed into one of the foremost and largest schools of its kind in the country - Red Bank School at Newton-le-Willows.

By May 1858 there were 138 boys on board the Akbar and 34 girls settling in at the other school, all considered to be progressing reasonably well. The Committee were thus sufficiently confident to start exploring the possibility of a Farm School type of Land Reformatory for the many boys of weak constitution who were totally unsuited for the rigours of training aboard the Akbar and the hardships of a future at sea. The Secretary observed: "Our work would be but half done unless a farm school type of land reformatory is established where such boys can be brought up and educated and the time spent in the fields will be of great benefit to the health of the many lads drawn from congested districts."

Apart from a few trials and anxieties of limited duration, the workings of the Liverpool Committee were on the whole blessed with good fortune. But their master stroke as regards the formative years of the farm school must surely have been when they asked Mr Richard Hughes Atty to scout nationwide for working details of other farm schools, and to deliver an outline plan as to how best one could be established and maintained. For this job he was paid £11 a month and travelling expenses, "the whole not to exceed £50," to cover the length of the country gleaning information from reformatory establishments as far away as Lambeth and Southampton before submitting his master plan in September 1858. The Committee were impressed with the result and he was given the task of finding, within three months, in the vicinity of Liverpool, a suitable farm school site at a price the Association could afford. The success of this mission won him the appointment of Superintendent at a salary of £120 a year with a house, coal and gas and three months' notice required on either side should the arrangement fail to work.

He was to remain as Head for 30 years, until his death at the age of 66 on September 15th 1888. As Superintendent he proved an excellent choice, and his total dedication and high standard of workmanship contributed greatly to the successful development of the farm school in its first stage. He demanded total self-restraint and, as a devout Christian, set a good example by his own conduct and demeanour. With his sincere combination of discipline, teaching and fatherly guidance, he was revered and respected by the majority of the lads, to the extent that a fair number of them in later years gave their sons his name.

When the situation required punishment with a heavy hand, Mr Atty could swish the rod without mercy, but there are, too, many examples in the old minute books which illustrate his fatherly care and kindness. Both he and his wife, who had no children of their own, took pity on a sickly consumptive boy and invited him to eat at their dining table to ensure that he received his fair amount of food. There was comfort also for a small, tearful boy

who had not heard from his father since arriving at the school. Wrote Mr Atty: "I called him to my room wiped away his tears and placed him by my knee. 'I hope soon to have a letter from your father and that he will be good to you,' I told him."
"The boy looked up and said: 'I have a good father.' 'Who is he?' I asked. 'You, Sir,' he said. With tears in my eyes I said to him: 'Go to bed and say a prayer to your Heavenly Father'."

He was held in high esteem by many of the old boys, who continued to correspond with him years after they had left the school. In their letters they poured out their secrets, their joys and their sadness. Wrote one: "My dear friend, I again take the pleasure of addressing a few lines to you, to maintain an intercourse which, though slight now, I hope will be eternal." After describing his grief at the loss of his first child, he went on: "You have not experienced the actual feelings of a parent, although you have always appeared to me to have a great love for children. The scriptural phrase 'like a father pitieth his children' often crosses my mind now and I find myself wondering if God really feels the same affection for me that I do for my little one. We had purposed calling our baby Richard Hughes as a slight token of affection for one who was a second father to me, but sad circumstances prevented this."

On his death bed Mr Atty was visited by several old boys. One of the last to see him alive was George, who later told his friends: "I was standing at the foot of the bed when Mr Atty opened his eyes and said: 'Gasking, are you a good lad?' I said: 'Yes Sir, I have kept the same place for two years.' Mr Atty replied: 'I hope I shall meet you in Heaven'."

His funeral was attended by the Committee, staff, the whole school and a large number of old boys. The coffin was carried by colleagues from the Church to the grave while the school band played the "Dead March" from "Saul". The bugles sounded the Last Post over the grave and many of the boys wept. Mr Atty is buried in St Peter's churchyard, less than a mile from the Red Bank School of today.

In their special tribute the Reformers noted: "The death of Mr Atty deprived the institution not merely of a superintendent, but of a father and one who, during his long connection with the school, threw such energy and devotion into his arduous duties. The thirty years he spent there were years of patient, persevering, faithful efforts to elevate the boys under his care above the influences of evil companionship and vice, and to implant principles of religion and virtue. He was successful in very numerous instances. His was a noble character."

Mrs Atty gave the boys a tea party with jam, bread and bunloaf before packing her trunks and heading for retirement in Southport.

Mr E Hampton Barclay answered the advertisement: *"Superintendent for Reformatory Farm School. Protestant and married. Salary £180 per year with house, coals and gas."* He was given the job.

Early Economies

When Mr Atty submitted his original plan in September 1858, the authorities moved quickly. The embryo of the Liverpool Farm School came into being that November, on the other side of the road from the Red Bank School of today and only a stone's throw from "Gallows Croft". A house, several outbuildings and a fair-sized acreage of land, well suited for the purpose intended, were leased for 10 years by the Liverpool Juvenile Reformatory Association at a rental of £120 a year for the house and £3 an acre for the land. Towards the end of that lease the present site was acquired and a new school built in 1867 at a cost of £3,500, made available on loan by Liverpool Corporation. By this time the Magistrates of the Borough had committed more than 506 boys and 107 girls to the Institutions of this Association alone. The boys, by helping with the road building, excavating and other labouring jobs, saved £50 in expenditure and the Committee agreed to pay £8 for an impressive and secure pair of iron gates and to cover the expense of a porch.

On April 27th 1868, Mr Atty, who had shouldered much of the responsibility, supervised the removal of the old school to the new site and was rewarded for his efforts with a generous bonus. The transfer was completed by the end of the week and the boys' accommodation increased from 98 to 125. In those days, the principal of the school was known as "Governor", and the approach to the school on Winwick Road, now the main A49, was little more than a cart track, with a cinder path on the left hand side. The four-sided block of the school, with one single lamp opposite the gate, was the only building in sight. Bridge Park became Liverpool Farm School in 1868 and remained so until 1950, when it was renamed Red Bank School.

The first boy to arrive at Bridge Park in the brooding monochrome gloom of a November morning was Nelson, a disobedient, spirited, Bluecoat schoolboy who was received as a free (uncommitted) case at the request of the Bluecoat Brotherly Society, who agreed to pay 4/- a week for four months towards his keep. Nelson was joined by William, a frail, pasty-faced little lad "too small for the Akbar", his father readily agreeing to contribute 3/6d a week, in the hope that the outdoor exertion would diminish the lad's evil exertions, bring a bloom to his cheeks and help to build up his muscles. Another early admission was a 12-year-old committed by the Stipendiary Magistrate as a "horse, ass, cow and cart stealer."

As a charitable organisation, the school had to be self-supporting in the early years and successful husbandry was of equal importance to the reformation of the young offenders. Top of the list of requirements for the new 32-acre farm school was the immediate purchase of a horse and cart. In addition, Mr Atty was authorised to buy 46 sheep costing £76 1s 1½d, to include 30

Small boys, some as young as 12, make their own boots under the eagle eye of an instructor at the Birkdale Farm School (1877-1900)

Older boys in the boot-making class, Birkdale Farm School

ewes to lamb in the spring; two additional horses, one at £30, the other at £24; two milk cows and one heifer. Five beehives were added at a later date.

The city boys worked hard on the land and their efforts contributed considerably towards the upkeep of the school. When good weather resulted in abundant crops, and the sale of farm produce and firewood soared, the lads earned a harvest treat and a half-day holiday.

By the end of 1859 the number of boys in school had increased to 16, and careful budgeting covered the salaries of a schoolmaster, paid yearly £60 with board; ploughman 16/- a week with cottage, gas and coals; gardener 21/- a week, and a female servant employed at £20 a year. Mr Atty, who agreed to manage the farm without any additional assistance "to save another salary", had his wage increased to £150 a year and the total outlay for staff earnings at the farm school for the year totted up to £326 4s. An old soldier attended once a week to drill the boys on military lines.

With the expansion of the school's aspirations expenses were high and the Committee, with the eye of a parsimonious bank manager, pruned every request for funds before agreeing to hand out one penny, whether it be for an additional horse or books for a library. Mr Atty's requests were, of necessity, numerous. He was authorised to spend only £5 on musical instruments for a drum and fife band. A plea for £20 to buy urgently needed library books was declared far too high and cut by £1. Badly needed additional accommodation for washing facilities was approved, providing the cost did not exceed £19.

Mr Atty readily adapted to his dual role as controller of wayward lads and tiller of the good earth. His duties were many and varied and even included keeping a book stating the daily work of the horse!

Harvest time was always a period of anxiety, as was evident in September 1860, when he gloomily reported that the weather was atrocious and had hindered the farm work. "The oats are housed and part of the wheat cut. The proceeds of the peas and beans are far short of hopes, the wet weather having caused many peas to rot on the ground, and the potatoes seem to be diseased." A month later the wheat had been secured and one third thrashed. After reserving enough for seed, 80 bushels were ready for market and there had been an offer of 60/- for 48 bushels. Ten lambs had been sold for £10, and 6 boys had received 12 strokes each on the back with a birch rod for pulling up and eating potato sets.

The farming enterprise see-sawed across the years, swinging between success and near disaster. It was reported in 1863: "Cheerful harvest news with all the stack hay sold for £3 10s per ton, and rhubarb at a good price." 1864: "A time of crisis. The cow has died suddenly, and I have been obliged to shoot the pony which has been lame in the leg while in the cart. Four pigs have died of distemper and it is necessary to buy 10 or 12 young beasts to consume hay and oat straw as it cannot be sold."

1889: "The past year has been disastrous. There was a loss on the farm, a decrease of £100 from the hire of boys and loss in the year's working, but the conduct of the boys has on the whole been satisfactory.

1890: "Sorry to have to report one of our cows in unwell. The mangle requires a complete overhaul, with your permission. One of our pigs has died of indigestion and a few boys have colds."

The farm, run on a stringent budget for much of the early years, proved a headache for all the superintendents, and in particular they deplored the cap-in-hand manner in which they were forced to appeal for extra equipment.

Making Ends Meet

The penny-pinching continued for many years. No-one escaped the frugality, not even the highly valued Medical Officer. For example, in the dawn of 1864 a quarter of the school occupants succumbed to colds and influenza, one boy was in hospital with acute diarrhoea and another seriously cut from a cross-saw. The rate of sickness in the previous year had been equally as demanding on the time and energy of the school doctor, with frequent calls on the ailing lads. His tentative inquiry regarding the possibility of an increase in his fees was refused, on the ground that he had shown no reason for such generosity, but owing to the volume of work during the previous year, he would receive an extra two guineas.

When the cooking range became too old and inadequate for the challenge of feeding the hungry lads, attempts were made to find an old ship's range as a replacement.

There was a rebuke for a coal delivery man in 1886: "In January we had three wagon loads; in February two, and now on 19th March, we are wanting a third. Going on as we are, four will hardly suffice for the month. The officer responsible complains that nearly one half is dust and drops through the bars. It seems incredible that the last two loads can have been screened, much less have passed over one. I should like to know how much would go through a pepper box before the quantity would be a fair price. Your people require telling and watching."

Three years later the Committee reluctantly agreed to purchase a cow and were profusely thanked by the Principal, who wrote: "I was so very glad to have your permission as the supply of milk is at present not sufficient."

The Committee vetted the account of every tradesman and the Superintendent was required to give a full explanation to every query raised. For example: October 10th 1890; I assure you that

I have endeavoured to get the tradesmen to send in their accounts every month in time for your meeting... Regarding the butcher's account, I shall look carefully over this to find out more about the charge of five-pence you complain about." "You will find the beef account greatly reduced as we have changed the supplier. I shall try to reduce the amount further. It is hardly fair to compare our school with Akbar as our numbers are lower and consequently cost more per head. Likely tinned meat is used on board. I must admit our cheese account is high, but we have not been using treacle lately, because we could not obtain it."

"My reason for changing from the China Tea Company, was because they charged us ninepence and elevenpence a pound for coffee which we had to mix and we could obtain better at tenpence a pound elsewhere. Perfume was got for the hospital when Cross was ill. The lump sugar Mrs Barclay ordered to make jam and jelly of the rhubarb which we could not sell and which is given to the boys from time to time. The paint I bought for the bath and renovating some beds. Is it all right for the Officers to pay two-and-a-half-penny per quart for milk or should we pay the outside price of threepence per quart?"

Occasionally the Superintendent rewarded himself with a pat on the back: March 6th 1893; "The account for the past year shows a balance to our credit of £197. This arises not so much from receipts derived from Industrial departments as from economy in the expenditure as will be seen by comparing 1891 with 1892. There is a saving of £119 in the provision account; £37 in clothing; £67 in fuel and light; £40 in medical. In fact all round there has been a reduction, except in rewards where there is an increase. This, of course, is owing to the improved conduct of the boys."

"When it is remembered that every boy has been clothed throughout with a new suit, cap, boots and three pairs of stockings, that their bedding has been improved, their food increased and £20 in extra prizes for awards, it will be seen that this reduction in the cost of maintenance is not produced at the expense of efficiency. Indeed, many of the boys have had two suits of clothing and two pairs of boots, owing to the wretched neglect of previous years."

Yet even in 1893 the farm was giving problems and it was reported: "At hay and harvest time we are very much at the mercy of our neighbours for cutting down the corn as we have no machine for this purpose. If the season should prove wet, as it has for the past two seasons, our crops are left to spoil because those who have a machine of their own require its use at the very time we need it. A mowing machine would be an acquisition to our stock. I recently bought an excellent plough, nearly new at a farm sale, I got it very cheap. This was greatly needed."

The high demand for firewood, which at that time was greater than the supply, was an important additional source of income. A request for a small engine to cut the wood more rapidly was at first refused, until a particularly good deal allowed the £20 cost to be repaid, half the money when the work began and the balance at the end of the year. By 1865 the sale of firewood had increased beyond all expectations and the go-ahead was given to buy 70 tons of old pine timber and 200 tons of good wood at 8/- a ton for chipping, and to consider establishing one of the boys with a donkey and cart at Southport, for the sale of firewood.

The proceeds of the enterprise increased over the years, showing a profit in 1865 of £116; in 1866, £127; 1867, £165 and in 1868, £192. School lessons suffered as the hours of instruction were slashed in favour of extra work, but no-one objected at top level when the Superintendent reported: "Pressure for firewood is so great we are compelled to reduce the school hours for dictation, ciphering, reading and arithmetic."

The new timetable meant that the boys were called at 5.15am and attended school from 6.00 to 7.15; they ate breakfast between 7.20 and 7.45, and chanted psalms and prayers until 8.00. Apart from a break between noon and 1.15 for dinner and play, the rest of the day was taken up by work until 4.45, when they washed and ate supper before attending school lessons between 6.00 and 7.00. A play hour followed and then half-an-hour of scripture and prayers before bed. On Tuesday and Thursday the late play

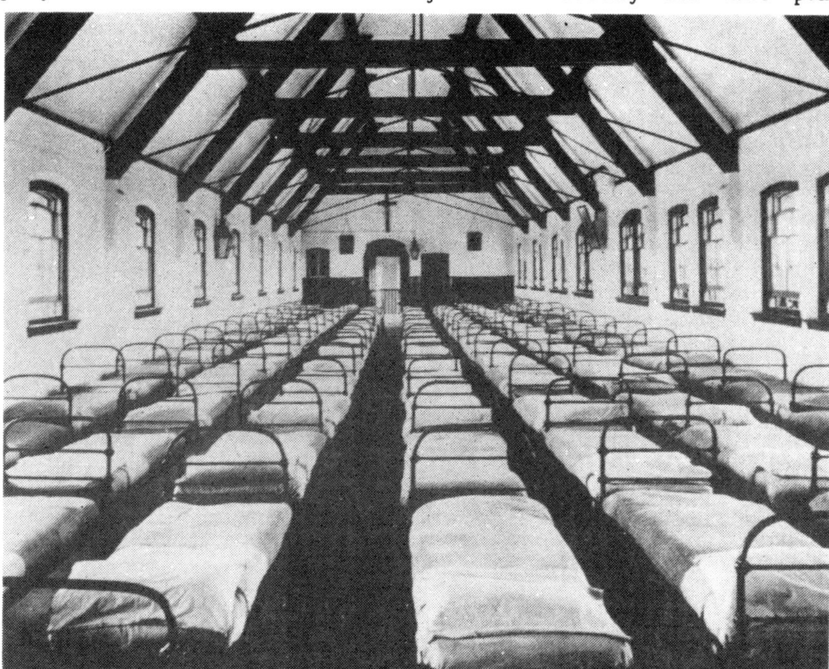

Boys' dormitory at the Birkdale Farm School

period was given up for band practice, and on Friday evening there was a singing lesson. Mr Atty reported: "When we get the work more advanced and some firewood in stock, we shall have the second division in school in the forenoon Tuesday, Wednesday and Thursday from 10.30 to noon, and the first division Monday and Friday from 3.30 to 4.45pm."

Wood chopping, paper bag making and similar non-educational employments were phased out in 1913 on the recommendation of the Departmental Committee of Reformatory and Industrial Schools. The group was the one set up two years earlier by Winston Churchill to investigate the organisation of Reformatory and Industrial Schools, staff qualifications and the after care of inmates.

The Committee's report made many important recommendations. Among other things, there were to be more highly qualified instructors and labour masters; future staff appointed should possess a Technical Certificate; for all children up to the age of 12 there should be full time schoolroom work, including suitable manual training; for children aged between 12 and 14 the system of "half time" in the school and "half time" in industrial training should be allowed, the children to spend at least 15 hours a week in the schoolroom unless a cut in hours was specially authorised by the Inspector; the hiring out of boys and girls was to be prohibited except in special cases with the consent of the Central Authority; there should be less tailoring and bootmaking in boys' schools and more training in the use of simple tools for wood and metal working.

In 1865 twenty of the trusted boys were employed in the village, returning each evening to the school for meals and to sleep. "With stronger and older boys we could have earned more," noted the Superintendent. Ten years later the number had increased to an outside workforce of 50 boys, bringing in a total income of £400 for the year. The scope of the work available improved as the years progressed and in 1897 boys hired out included a lad who worked for a baker, earning 9/- a week; Henry, employed by a printer at 6/- a week; George, who earned 12/- a week at the Sugar Works, and William, hauling coal for a local merchant at 9/- a week. Several of the boys worked at the colliery.

All forms of monetary support were gratefully received by the hard-up reformers and an offer by Mr Alan Potter of five guineas for the shooting rights over the farm in May 1865 was readily accepted, with the proviso that the Reverend Mr Carter, Chaplain of the Borough Gaol, be permitted the privilege of an occasional day's shooting also.

Keeping in Touch

Included in Mr Atty's onerous duties was responsibility for supervising the licensing of the boys, visiting their homes and workplaces upon discharge and reporting on their progress. In addition he had to cope with a mountain of correspondence, penning all the letters by hand. He neatly recorded in September

1868: "I visited twentyfive lads and found all but two to be working well, but I was so displeased with the state of Mrs O'Brien's lodging house in Smithfields that I have complained to the Health Committee."

In 1904 the Superintendent reported on visits to 16 boys in South Wales, London and Devonshire, where he found them to be working satisfactorily with good reports from their masters. Two of the lads had been in the same situation for four years and eight for two years.

For boys with no roots or those alienated from their families the school's own particular combination of parental discipline and care inevitably forged a strong bond of attachment between reformer and delinquent. On special occasions or when times were hard, the link drew the lads back to the school like a magnet. Forty-nine discharged youths visited in 1877. One proudly displaying his second mate's certificate stayed a week, and a Royal Artilleryman with no family or friends spent his furlough at the school. In March 1900, Bertie deliberately stole a muffler to ensure his return, and three boys from bad homes, out of work and fearful of being picked up by the police for loitering, were re-admitted.

There were times, however, when the bonding created problems. In 1887 the Superintendent stated: "We have been troubled with

Physical instruction for Birkdale Farm School boys. Midriff bulge was due to the availability of kit in one size only, which meant the boys had to roll over the spare material

visits from many of the old lads unemployed. Lads very anxious a short time since to get away are now haunting the School more than we like or than is good for them."

In 1932, an old boy who had been discharged 22 years earlier wrote a desperate letter from Pimlico, London: "As an old school-boy, can you help me to get some clothing and food. I am out of employment and in receipt of a disability pension of eight shillings a week for life, but that had to go for rent. My wife is an invalid and my daughter incapacitated through defective eyesight. Trusting you will do your best for me." Sadly there was little that the Superintendent could do to help and he replied: "I very much regret that I cannot offer you anything as we are similarly situated ourselves and I am absolutely fixed with boys who are here with time expired and I cannot find them employment."

There was no sympathy for the laggard. Idle boys who seriously threatened to abuse the farm school hospitality were sent packing in 1891. Superintendent John Digwood reported: "Some few worthless lads have made the school their place of refuge when idle and too lazy to work, but, as their example and influence were pernicious, I assisted them to other fields to try their fortune."

Hospitality was extended to old boys at Christmas and holidays, and many sat down to a Christmas Day feast of hot-pot and plum pudding, and received the highly-prized gift of an orange and apple which they would not otherwise have enjoyed. They attended morning service and remained on into the evening to watch the musical concert and magic lantern display, and to sing songs grouped around the candlelit Christmas tree. It was a joyous occasion and in later years, in letters from America, India and far away points of the British Empire, old boys recalled their Christmas Day at the farm school, and wrote of their "grateful remembrance".

There was always a warm welcome for the returning hero and a receptive audience of wide-eyed lads to hear him relate his tale of bravery and initiative. Such a hero was James, who visited in 1915 on sick leave from the Front. His gallantry had won him the DCM at Zonnebeke.

The system which gave so many of the reformatory boys the opportunity to do something useful with their lives inspired in them a loyalty towards the younger boys who were in the process of their reformation. There are many examples of generous donations and practical help. In 1889 old boys on the ships Lolla Rook, Shakespear, Dovenby, Archer and Cockermouth sent money. The earnest spirit of Victorian philanthropy was communicated to the reformatory boys and girls and there are several examples of them digging into their meagre mark money or earnings to make donations for Indian Famine Relief or, nearer to home, for the destitute of Lancashire.

The Emigrants

Old boys who had settled successfully abroad helped to pave the way for lads wishing to emigrate by forwarding passage money and finding jobs for them when they arrived.

Francis, once a skinny Liverpool vagrant picked up by the police as he huddled under a railway arch for protection from the bitter night frost, remembered with appreciation the system which taught him to read and write and convinced him that, although he had entered this world as a nobody's child, he had a Heavenly Father who, aided by the reformatory system, would guide and help him to prove his worth if he were honest, obedient and industrious. Francis emigrated to America in 1872. Eight years later he was a prosperous businessman in the Mid West, sent a $20 bill to the farm school and found jobs for two boys in America.

Emigration was the answer for many of the lads when local work opportunities slumped. The administration involved in the emigration of a reformatory lad was considerable and added yet another burden to the workload of the superintendent, who was responsible for much of the organisation involved. This was evident in a letter dated April 7th 1886, from Mr Atty to the Reverend J Bridger, Chaplain to Emigrants for the Society for the Propagation of the Gospel:

"Dear Sir: I hear you sail on the 22nd May in the Allen Steamer Circassia and I am sending two lads under your care for work in Ontario or Manitoba. Henry, aged 19, is a Confirmed lad and entirely friendless. He is a healthy hardy lad, accustomed to farm work, can milk and handle a horse and use a spade. Horatio, aged 18, is also a strong healthy lad and has had care of the cows and pigs, and is at present shippon boy. He has drunken parents."

"I should like to get them to farm work. We have an old lad, now father of a family and in a responsible situation, in charge of a length of railway in County Peel, Ontario. If we could get them into that neighbourhood, I should be glad, but defer to your greater knowledge."

"Is it possible tc get a good map or maps of Canada large enough to find a county in? I have a Philips Handy General Atlas - which is too crowded and gives nothing west of Lake Huron. The two boys you took out last year are doing well. It would be grand to send a third lad, but his parents object, so there is an end of the matter. It is time he was away from school and he tells me he can get work at Mr Leach's Sugar Works."

"I presume you would rather I paid their fares to Allen's at their office. Will you kindly say whether I should pay through to

Manitoba? The further away, the less likely they are to return. under a spasm of worklessness or homesickness. But where you think you can dispose of them best is the main consideration. So will you kindly say Manitoba or Toronto."

In a second letter dated April 21st 1886, Mr Atty wrote to the Reverend Bridger on board ship. "I have told the lads to give this to you when at sea, and you have a little leisure. May you have a pleasant voyage and a happy Eastertide. Each of the lads has a Post Office order for a pound, payable at Winnipeg, from me Robert Atty, in their names. If they are perplexed to cash it, you will perhaps kindly advise them. They have also money with them, half a sovereign each, besides silver, how much I don't know, to keep them on the railway. Henry, the bigger of the two, is fond of gambling! May all go well with you and the lads."

The magnetic appeal of gambling, and the ease with which lads were robbed of money and even clothing during a game of chance set up by the wily crew of an emigration ship, caused the Committee to think again about the timing of each boy's gift of survival money. Hearing that their £5 donation to each farm school boy en route to a new life in Australia was usually lost to sailors in a game of Crown and Anchor, a group of kindly philanthropic gentlemen from Huyton instructed that the money must be given to the lads at the end of the voyage.

Emigration was also the answer for many a troublesome boy who, without doubt, would have followed a downward path of transgerssion had he remained in this country under the bad influence of family and friends. Typical of these was Morgan. Reported Mr Atty: "His conduct whilst in the school has certainly not been good and if he returns to Liverpool, it is more than probable that he will get into trouble. At the same time he is a good working lad and has a better knowledge of farm work than any boy we have here."

"His mother, who is a widow with several children, is very anxious for the sake of the rest of the family, as well as the boy, that he be sent away and she would contribute as much as she is able for this purpose." Morgan was shipped to Canada with William, a well-behaved lad, quite friendless, with no prospect of obtaining employment at home. It was hoped that they might turn out as well as old boy Gray, who had emigrated to Beaver Creek, Columbia, Canada, and finished up a soldier in the Salvation Army! Gray was considered far more of a success than the old boy who, in 1887, wrote an article in Harper's magazine under the heading of "The route of the wild Irishman".

In those days, the mental acumen of the emigrant appeared to have little bearing on the decision to ship him. For example, on July 4th 1887 Richard sailed to Pennsylvania at his father's expense. Mr Atty remarked: "He is a simple little fellow and said to me, 'Good bye, I am sorry you are bad. God bless you, I will say my prayers for you'."

Under the supervision of schoolmaster Mr Needham, Henry was allowed to say goodbye to his parents in Liverpool before embarking. They were hardly worthy of such consideration, having in the previous year accepted their boy on licence, pawned the new clothes he had brought with him, and drunk the profit before turning him out on to the streets. Picked up by the police, Henry was re-committed by Mr Raffles, the Stipendiary Magistrate. Mr Needham paid to get the clothing out of pawn, secured the passage ticket and handed Henry into the care of the Reverend Bridger to sail for a new life in Canada.

There were times when the superintendent doubted a lad's willingness to succeed in a new life abroad, and this lack of confidence was expressed in a letter from Mr Atty to a prospective employer who wrote from Canada for a lad to work in his flour mill. "Brown, aged 19 is a strong, healthy, active lad, anxious to emigrate and I expect there would be no home difficulties. The Miller who has had more to do with him than anyone else, speaks very well of him, but neither Mrs Atty nor I, nor the Schoolmaster have the same confidence."

"He is a rough, boorish sort of boy and though he declares he has given up the use of tobacco, I am doubtful. Here he is forced to abstain, but whether he will do so when free, I cannot say, but rather think not. I don't anticipate his becoming a drunkard, but I doubt he is as thrifty and prudent as to deny himself either tobacco or beer, for the sake of future advantage. I have two or three lads of very different manners and habits, suitable as regards character, but they have not worked at the Mill. So I fear we must lose for them the good opportunity and Brown must take his chance."

Not all the boys settled abroad and there were several examples of chances thrown aside. In January 1893 two farm school lads, sent to Canada the previous spring, returned. The Superintendent noted: "One of the boys visited at Christmas and said he had not liked the climate. Unfortunately other Reformatories have had similar experiences, which in some measure is attributed to the alteration of the law requiring boys to be discharged before emigrating."

Mr Atty expected every boy to report on his progress in the ensuing years and when this was not done, he expressed his disappointment: "Holland has not written home for some time, certainly not since he became a father. I should be glad to have a letter from him, but having a wife and child, I expect he has no time. I got very much attached to him and I hope that he is a Christian. He is with a farmer in Winnipeg."

The most rewarding letters for the Reformers must have been those like the following, from sixteen-year-old John Bliss. Discharged from Saltney Reformatory, Birmingham, to sail from Liverpool on board the steam ship Sarmatian on June 25th 1875 for a new life in Canada, he wrote to the Superintendent: "Many thanks for teaching me what you have. I am working for a kind old gentleman and he likes me very much. I am up at 5 o'clock morning, milking cows, feeding horses, work in the fields harvesting. I have fell in with a few friends who came out of the old country. My master had me a week on trial, after, he wanted to hire me for the year, he asked me how much I wanted. I told him eight dollars per month, so he said I was too strong, so I said seven. I told him I would try to do my best and so I have.

"I have all kinds of nice things to eat, such as custard, cherry pie, jam tart, milk, tea or coffee every meal whichever I like, and as much bacon, and meat as I like. If ever you tell the boys this it will make their mouths water. I am happy as the day is long.

"Men are looking for boys every day and I am sure that if the boys meant to stop over here they would soon get a farm of their own. Married men are allowed two hundred acres of land, single men over eighteen years of age one hundred."

A Strict Discipline

The system which then controlled the farm school boys was a unique combination of harsh unbending discipline, inflexible in its response to bad behaviour, and an earnest paternal concern for their welfare. The bad were so severely punished that their fear of the consequences discouraged a repeat performance. The good flourished, and their progress through life was charted with pride by those involved in their reformation. The whole reflected in 1889 a success rate of 78½%. In 1902 the percentage or re-conviction recorded was 3.22, the lowest rate in the history of the school.

Before the introduction of the mark system, birching and flogging were the order of the day for villainous conduct. Unlawful wounding, "High Rip", as it was known in those days, brought retribution of the severest type. On September 12th 1887, Mr Atty recorded: "There have been some indications of the High Rip. For using a knife on another boy's neck, I confined Robert in the cell and he was soundly birched."

"George, out on licence, has been very troublesome, becoming acquainted with a girl and some ill-conditioned lads, and apparently an admirer of High Rips. He beat two maid girls at the house of his employer, and threatened a respectable washer-woman with a knife and, I understand, rather frightened them. He was brought back, surly and unrepentant, and given twelve on the back with a birch rod in public. When let down in the hearing of the whole school he said 'I will have my revenge'. He was then immediately hoisted on the back of another lad and got twelve more. I have to confess transgression of the rule relative to flogging, but trust the Committee will condone it. I am hopeful that the lads have learned that those who hanker after the fame of the High Rip, will have to pull down their breeches."

Floggings were recorded for the theft of one pennyworth of sweets, blackberrying, bird nesting, killing a duck, scrumping apples, idleness and smoking. A persistent absconder received 18 lashes instead of the routine 12. For theft and persistent absconding, lads appeared before the Stipendiary Magistrate and were ordered three months in prison or released to enlist.

The Committee and HM Inspectors carefully monitored all punishment and a labour master could lose his job for doling out unfair or excessive chastisement. In 1900 an Assistant Master lost his £70-a-year appointment with rooms and coals for knocking a boy's head against a desk and blackening the eye of another lad who had stepped out of line. A teacher who failed to record his punishment of two boys was officially reprimanded and ticked off for using a small willow instead of a cane or strap.

The mark system was introduced in 1896. It was a revolutionary step forward as it lessened corporal punishment and, it was hoped, would act as a stimulus towards better conduct. It worked on the basis that a total of 300 marks divided between good conduct, school lessons and industrial work would be given to each boy at the beginning of every quarter, with the object that he should lose as few marks as possible.

The scale for rewards was as follows. The loss of 140 out of 300 was "fair" with 1/- reward; 100 "very fair" - 2/-; 60 "good" - 2/6d; 30 "very good" - 3/-, while the loss of only five marks was "excellent" and rewarded the well-behaved lad with 3/6d.

For the boy who had been in the school nine months and had totted up 500 marks there was permission to wear one stripe; eighteen months at school with an additional 700 marks in credit, two stripes; two years and three months and an additional 700 marks, three stripes. A triple entry on the "Excellent List" rewarded a boy with a gold stripe and a cut in his detention time of one month. For six times on the "Excellent List" in two years, a boy had his sentence reduced two months and for being listed nine times in three years, three months. Boys who had been in school for three years without meriting a good conduct stripe had to remain until they succeeded or as long as the law would allow.

Observed the Superintendent in 1897: "At first the boys seemed to think it was a good joke to have a few marks stopped for an offence when formerly they got the cane. When they realised that loss of marks meant loss of money, leave, stripes and other privileges, they became more interested, and now they scan the good conduct list anxiously to learn how they stand at the end of each quarter."

During the ensuing nine months 129 boys were punished. Eleven of them were flogged, 55 caned, the cells were used on four occasions and the remainder of the boys lost marks. The most notable feature was the diminution in the number of times the same boys had offended.

Records were carefully kept of the "Moral" return of the lads. For the three years ending 1874, of 116 discharged boys, 94 were reported to be doing well, 1 doubtful, 13 convicted, including 3 discharged to penal servitude, and of the 8 unknown, 1 boy had been sent to San Francisco, another to St Louis and one lad absconded and stowed away to America after only one day in school and was never heard of again.

Parental Concern

Every effort was made to protect the boys, aged 10 to 16, from the slightest taint of degeneracy. Their reading matter was carefully censored and swearing severely punished. At the turn of the century, an angry letter was despatched to the Clerk of the Council objecting to the placing of a public seat opposite the front entrance of the Farm School and in particular to the characters who lingered there.

"I regret to say this seat is becoming a nuisance to the Institution, and a source of menace to its well-being. It is frequently occupied by tramps and others of a very undesirable type, and, during the evening, by youths who make even Sunday evening hideous with all the latest Music Hall ditties, many with variations of a more or less degenerate character. As our dormitories and schoolroom overlook this spot, I should consider it a favour if this seat could be removed to a more suitable place. I feel sure that the Council would not willingly encourage anything likely to increase the difficulty of maintaining proper discipline in such an Institution as this, or of hampering the endeavours to promote a healthy moral tone amongst the inmates. I trust this appeal from an Institution which pays a considerable proportion of rates to the Urban District Council, will receive early and favourable consideration."

An application by the mother of George for his return to her on licence was agreed on the understanding that he should not live at the public house of which she was manager, and in 1890, Harold was "thankfully discharged" to enlist in the 8th King's Warrington Regiment, to avoid his return to Liverpool, where his home was "of the very worst kind".

Extracts from the Superintendent's correspondence books over the years revealed many examples of fatherlike concern and interest in the wellbeing of the boys whilst on licence and in later years. Mr Atty noted in April 1886: "A very engaging little boy, Alfred Moran, is very ill with pneumonia. He says his parents have left where they lived and have never written to him. I am anxious that the mother and father should know and shall write to the old address, chancing delivery."

"The other evening he told my wife: 'One night when my father, mother and auntie were drinking, I cuddled in a corner of the staircase out of the way and fell asleep. Mother coming up stairs saw me and said "Here's our Alf, he could sleep on a clothes line".' I should not like to be the parent of a child with that picture printed on its memory as it passes into the unknown."

The Superintendent wrote to Mrs Moran: "I am sorry to tell you your son is very ill with pneumonia. He is well attended. He tells me you have shifted and have never written to him, so I fear this may not reach you."

In another letter to Miss Fanny Smith, he wrote: "Your brother, Thomas, is dangerously ill with broncho-pneumonia, developing typhoidal complications. Yesterday his temperature was 105. We gave him quinine every two hours and sprayed him with cold water and at 5.15 this morning brought down his temperature to 100. The temperature is rising again. He is very weak and occasionally delirious and has been visited three times a day by the Medical Officer. He would be glad to see you - his mother has not yet written."

It was not unusual for a lad to be abandoned by uncaring parents, thankfully shelving their responsibility on to the reformers. On May 3rd 1890, a letter was sent to Mrs Kelly: "I am sorry to say your nephew, Albert, is sinking fast. He wrote to his father some time ago, but has not received a reply. I shall be obliged by your letting his father know, so that he may visit him as soon as possible." Arthur, who went to Canada in 1870, appealed to the school to try to find out about his parents, from whom he had not heard since emigrating.

Had it not been for the concern of the system, many of those who died through ill health would certainly have finished up in a pauper's grave. Such a lad would have been Peter Jackson, who died from meningitis on May 8th 1890. No-one from his family turned up to attend his funeral in Newton Churchyard. The Superintendent organised an impressive and loyal service with himself and the boys in attendance and the school band playing the "Dead March". Another sick boy on licence sought re-admission to be nursed and to die at the school. Six spaces were purchased at Newton cemetery by the reformers and there remain to this day, two graves with room for three boys each.

For the poor but supportive parent help was available. When John, "a quiet, well-behaved lad and well liked by everyone," was killed at the sawmill where he worked, the Reformers paid his funeral expenses of £2 10s to help his "very decent but very poor mother." Officers and boys also made a subscription for her. A mother who travelled a great distance to be with her dying son was allowed to stay at the school to enable her to attend his burial.

A reconciliation between parent and wayward son was a joyous occasion. Henry, the son of a well-to-do tradesman from a respectable city suburb, was thankfully discharged when his parents agreed to have him home again, believing him to be a changed boy. At the age of ten the lad had been brought before the magistrates for a minor misdemeanour and his parents, feeling so keenly the disgrace, had then refused to have anything to do with him.

Mr Atty reported on a similar act of forgiveness: "Six months since Nathaniel was prosecuted by his father, whose heart was turned from him, and he deplored that he had brought the lad into the world. This Christmas his parents, stirred by the Christian message, came to see him and brought with them a fine parcel. They are by God's mercy at one again."

Diet, Disease and Disaster

Many of the lads who arrived at the farm school in the early days were "poor starved little creatures". On their limited budget the Reformers, under the watchful eye of HM Inspector, made every effort to provide the boys with a dietary programme which, although spartan, would keep them reasonably healthy.

The boys made their own bread in 1890. Bread formed a high percentage of the rations in the Reformatory Institutions in those early days and the nutritious content was important and under frequent review.

In 1898, HM Inspector T D Robertson paid a surprise visit to the school and watched the boys hungrily tucking into their dinner of 12 ounces of bread and two ounces of cheese, washed down by a pint of cocoa. The dinner menu at that time varied little, and the improvements which resulted from the Inspector's visit must have been very welcome to the ravenous lads.

Reformatory lads baking bread for school use

They each had for Sunday dinner a pie containing 5oz meat, 4oz flour and 12oz potatoes; this was followed on Monday with one pint of soup made from bones, peas and vegetables and 8oz bread; Tuesday - 1 lb suet pudding with raisins; Wednesday - a stew of 6oz meat, 12oz potatoes, pot herbs and 4oz bread; Thursday ; 1 lb suet pudding with treacle or stewed rhubarb; Friday - a meat and potato pie, the same as on Sunday; Saturday - 12oz bread, 2oz cheese and 1 pint of cocoa. Each boy latterly was taught to use a knife and fork correctly; in the early days he had only a spoon.

In 1903, cooked fish was served twice a week and by 1914 the farm school was using 250 pounds of "boys" beef and bullock heads each week.

In 1912, the opinion of the County Analyst was sought as to the suitability of the bread they gave to their "growing lads". The baker was under contract to supply bread consisting of two sacks of best seconds flour to one sack of best thirds. The charge per hundred 4 lb loaves was 32/- less 5% discount, the price to include delivery. The County Analyst found the sample genuine in accordance with specifications but considered it to be somewhat heavy. He advised that the flour used should be well mixed.

Few of the boys admitted were glowing with good health. Lousy lads had their heads shaved and washed with carbolic. Scrofulous lads were given extra food. Lads with ringworm and the prevalent eye infections were isolated.

In the early months of 1891, 50 boys and nearly all the officers and Superintendent were ill with influenza. Epidemics of scarlet fever, measles, diphtheria and the occasional case of osteomyelitis were of great concern.

"Much wanted is a detached Infirmary where such cases can be isolated," stressed the Superintendent in March 1880. Orphaned and friendless lads with illnesses of a malignant nature were discharged to the Workhouse Infirmary.

A newspaper statement in October 1900 quoted the anger of Stipendiary Magistrate Mr Stewart, directed at the Liverpool Reformers, who had turned down one of his committals and accused them of "picking only healthy boys". This was contested vigorously, the Superintendent retaliating with details of some of the cases received at his schools from Mr Stewart's court. Lads who, according to the Superintendent, placed the system at great disadvantage particularly when they were put out on licence. The list included: Number 1357: Deformed foot - was placed out to tailoring. 1448: Deformed foot - also suffering from eczema and ringworm in the hand and deplorably emaciated; it took several months to cure him. 1369: Chronic bronchitis. 1377: Of weak intellect, licensed to parents at their request after 18 months, parents well able to look after him. 1399: Double hernia, weak intellect and unfit for work, can do little with him. 1428: Strumous and debilitated, still under treatment. 1437: Consumptive, lately treated for pneumonia. 1470: Neglected scabies, isolated for a month after admission. 1476: Diseased kidneys, much debilitated, put to bed on admission. 1494: Acute gonorrhoea, discharged, "this beastly case I had to attend to myself". 1408: Catarrh and acute scabies, police doctor reported he would require supervision.

"Case 1182: Was accepted at the request of the Stipendiary Magistrate, although suffering from consumption of the bowels and was a most offensive case requiring my special care. Our school receives all the boys not physically fit for the Akbar; consequently we get the refuse of a class of boys whose physical stamina is of the lowest type. With regard to the lad referred to by the Stipendiary Magistrate, although I had no room for him - having 150 boys - I told the officer who brought him that if he were passed by the doctor, I would make room available by putting a boy on licence. To say the least, it is unfair to fill our school with boys unfit for industrial training and who cannot be fitted for any useful occupation in life, while more suitable lads are left to run the streets because no school can be found for them. I appreciate Mr Stewart's difficulty; it is bad to send back such helpless lads to their squalid surroundings."

"What is really wanted is a Government Convalescent Reformatory, to which all such lads unfitted for ordinary Reformatories could be sent. At present we have a boy with one arm, another with a deformed foot, a third with both feet almost crippled. Although glad to do what we can for these poor lads, we must draw a line somewhere, otherwise we shall have a lot of boys on our hands and not be able to do anything for them. If Mr Stewart's ruling is to hold good, I am afraid that an Infirmary will have to be built and a qualified nurse added to our staff."

The Superintendent was instructed that no boy in future should be received until passed by the Medical Officer as physically and mentally fit and free from tuberculin taint.

The problem of keeping the lads fit was a headache for the authorities and the Inspectors were always on the lookout for possible sources of infection. On August 11th 1898, HM Inspector Walsh called attention to the ventilation holes bored in the floors of two dormitories as a source of "generating fever and breeding microbes" and suggested their removal; he also recommended boarding in the damp walls of the dining room.

Fourteen years earlier, after several of the 133 boys at the farm school had become ill with fever and one had died from typhoid, official concern was centred on sewage from Earlestown which was being carried into Newton Brook and thus past the back of the school. There was particular concern for the health of the boys employed at the farm Mill, which dated back to the time of Cromwell, and the Medical Officer suggested that the brook should be thoroughly flushed out in cold weather by opening the sluices, when the flood water would create an overflow of Newton Mere, releasing many tons per minute. He remarked philosophically:

"The boys who work on the farm and about the Mill are neither the youngest nor the weakest. They take a lot of fresh air with the poison and, most probably, they become acclimatised." The surveyor of the Newton Commissioners made his own investigation and admitted that the action of the chemical used at the nearby paper works on the filtered sewage caused the excreta to separate and that this, together with the filth from the works, polluted the stream.

A large sum was spent on improving the situation. The Earlestown open drain was covered up, a closed drain installed and the source of danger to the health of the farm school finally removed. The following year the Superintendent reported that the boys were in better health than in previous years and no deaths had been recorded.

A good well and rain collected in barrels constituted the sole water supply for the school at the outset, and it was not until 1880 that this was augmented from the town water works, after Mr Atty reported the well supply greatly reduced, and suggested a fire engine to enable them to use water from the outside bathing pit for washing. As an economy measure the school continued to rely considerably on the untapped water. In 1886, the Superintendent wrote: "Rain is wanted. I do not know what we should have done but for the open air bath and the water barrels."

In January 1893, when the Newton Commissioners increased their water charges 100%, from 6d to 1/- per 1,000 gallons, the school was ordered to economise further.

Standards of general hygiene and cleanliness gradually improved. Separate towels greatly reduced the number of boys with eye infections in 1895 and each lad was given his own toothbrush. Infected clothing was stoved and towels boiled. At the same time HM Inspector recommended extra warm clothing, flannel singlets, with the shirt lined over the chest and the back down to the waist, and a new blanket for each boy "as two of the three they have are of little use as regards warmth." Heating was installed in the dormitory and the schoolroom for the younger boys, and three years later, when all the dormitories were fitted with steam pipes, making them cosy and comfortable, fewer boys absconded during the winter months.

Apart from the heavy toll of sickness which at times necessitated the hiring of a nurse, many of the lads were accident prone. In 1891, Thomas lost the ends of his left thumb and forefinger after striking a small dynamite cap with a hammer, playing about in the shoemaker's shop. Jackson swallowed a piece of chewing tobacco and felt no ill effects until early the following morning when he was seized with violent pains of the heart and vomiting. Prompt measures were taken and for a few hours he remained in a critical condition before recovering. Henry met with an accident while working the circular saw and the doctor was obliged to take off his thumb. John lost two fingers in the corn crusher and Nelson broke two fingers working at the printing works. The scullery boy scalded his foot, Charles broke his arm while cleaning out the pig sty and Batley was killed greasing a machine at the printing works. A workman, thinking he was at the water closet, started the machine, killing the lad instantaneously.

There remains to this day a memorial stone marking the spot where one boy was struck by lightning. The Superintendent reported: "An innocent, merry lad, during a lull in a thunder-storm left the school gate with milk for the ploughman and in the open field was struck dead by a flash of lightning. A stone worked and lettered by one of our lads as a labour of love marks the spot."

A similar chapter of disaster was recorded in an earlier year. In one week the Superintendent recorded: "A fine lad, John William, affectionate, honest, willing, industrious and brave, lost his life falling from the roof of the building where he climbed unknown to any of the officers to recover a sweep's brush. The following day two old boys were killed by the explosion in the Wood Pit, and a third, hurled by the fierce blast against the wall at the mouth of the shaft, remembers when the blast struck him crying out in his agony: 'God, forgive me I have been very wicked,' before becoming unconscious." "On the same day a boy fell while running in the yard and put out his hip-joint."

The Daily Round

Before the late 1920's the farm school boys wore a "uniform" of scarlet and blue serge, styled with brass buttons, stripes down the trousers and an Eton jacket. Several attempts were made over the years to make the uniforms less institutionalised. Such a venture in 1897 brought a rebuke from HM Inspector: "Uniforms are an absolute necessity in schools of our class and are our special safeguard against absconding. If we change the design of our coats it will be necessary to wear collars which will make more washing and I see no advantage to be gained from a change - our boys seem to be proud of their uniform."

The material was extremely hard wearing and in 1887 cost 3/5d a yard for a double width. A "Sunday" suit was introduced in later years, based on a specimen which passed the test of being worn daily for a year without "costing sixpence for repairs," retained its colour and was still wearable after being passed on by two more boys. It was of medium weight and very suitable for summer and winter. There was an additional advantage, for when a boy left school he was supplied with two suits of clothes. Already equipped with a Sunday suit, he would need only one and there would be the added incentive for him to take more care of his Sunday clothes.

Apart from animal husbandry and growing crops and vegetables, the boys had an opportunity of learning a trade. There was a tailor's shop, where they spent much of their time sewing by hand until 1901 when a sewing machine was purchased, a shoe making department, joinery, baking, and in 1904, plumbing was included with glazing and slating. Some of the articles sold for domestic use were kitchen tables, boxes, barrows, seats and dog kennels. The practical work produced was of a good quality and examples won prizes at the "City and Guilds of London" and the "Union of Lancashire & Cheshire Institutes".

In 1896 there were 34 boys employed on the farm, 10 in the garden, greenhouses and cucumber-houses, 5 in the Mill, 3 in the bakery, 7 in joinery, 30 with the tailor, 10 knitting and mending, 13 with the shoemaker, 6 in the house and laundry, 28 in the brass band and 31 working out at the printing works as half-timers.

With a view to encouraging some of the more promising boys to further proficiency in their trade, a system of apprenticeship was tried for a time in 1900. The lads received a wage, were lodged in the school in separate accommodation and came under less rigid discipline. When they were capable of doing journeymen's work, they joined local builders and tradesmen, returning to the school each evening.

School subjects covered composition, recitation, mental arithmetic, reading, writing, geography, drawing and map study. The British Empire was singled out for special study. There were two excellent bands, a string band and a brass and reed band, which was always kept at a high pitch of efficiency and was rewarded with a good tea at local functions of note after

Classroom at Birkdale Farm School, 1900

entertaining the crowds. It cost three guineas to hire the band of 30 youths and bandmaster for a procession timed between 1.45pm and 3.30pm. This charge was increased to five guineas if the organisers required the band to play through to 7.30pm. The Superintendent replied to one applicant: "We shall be quite willing to play at your Gymkhana on the day and times stated. Our terms are five-guineas and you would be required to supply a substantial tea. Please let me know early if this is acceptable, as there is a great demand for the Band during June."

In the three years prior to 1900, 14 boys from the brass section joined Army bands. At that time there were 21 old boys serving in South Africa, one of whom returned to the battle after being shipped home to recuperate from his wounds. The school was run on almost military lines, with "square bashing" and band playing. The march to church in four companies on a Sunday would have won the approval of the most unyielding of sergeant majors!

The reformers, fully aware that when creativity is turned inward and suppressed it often explodes violently and destructively, allowed no lad to idle. When severe weather prevented outdoor work, the boys were given extra lessons and domestic duties. An offer in 1890 for the boys to sort paper at 5/- a ton was gladly accepted with the comments: "It will prove nice employment for the farm boys on wet days, keeping them occupied and it will make work for the younger ones."

Highlights and Holidays

Highlight of all the treats was on the days when the harshest of winter weather frosted the Newton lake into a giant ice-sliding playground. On January 9th 1893 the whole school enjoyed this pleasurable experience and, although the majority of boys suffered from chilblains as a result, their discomfort was considered well worth the joy of the sport.

The early days were particularly monotonous for high-spirited lads with limited recreational facilities. An American organ, donated to the school, kept them in tuneful harmony at morning and evening songs of praise and prayers. For added cheer, the Chaplain attended twice a week to join in the boys' games and exercises and was "a kindly and wholesome influence". The Church of England Temperance Society founded a branch at the school, with three of the officers and several of the older boys taking the abstinence pledge, and there were regular lectures on the subject.

Important visitors caused a buzz of excitement and were greeted with the sort of welcome and awe usually reserved for Royalty. The Annual Prize Distribution Day was always graced with an eminent guest. In 1896 the Earl of Derby visited to present prizes for good conduct, religious knowledge, schoolwork and neatness, and one little fellow rejoiced that he had shaken hands with His Lordship three times, having received an equal number of prizes.

The Governor of the Isle of Man visited in June 1880 and various Lord Mayors of Liverpool presented prizes over the years. The farm school was never honoured by some of the Royal visitors and celebrities who were attracted to the Akbar, but no visitors to the farm school were more warmly welcomed than Miss Champney and Miss Claughton who, in the dreary early days, called regularly to hear the boys repeat scriptures and reward them with home-made gingerbread! Other lady visitors knitted chest protectors and provided nourishing treats for the weakly boys.

In 1916 good lads were allowed small parcels from home. Bad boys forfeited this privilege. The Superintendent wrote to the mother of one such boy: "Dear Madam, I regret to inform you that your son has again been in trouble. This is his second offence since he left. He does not as yet seem to be reformed and at Court this morning the Justices deemed it advisable for him to be returned to the School."

"I sincerely hope that you will co-operate with me in seeing that he gets his proper punishment, and I suggest that you do not send any parcels or visit him for a time, so that he will feel it. This might be conducive to his good behaviour in the future."

Twenty-seven boys whose names appeared on the "good conduct" list in 1889 were allowed out to watch the Crowning of the Rose Queen at Golborne. Feast days and holidays were marked in a special way, either by a sports day with racing, jumping and swimming and a donation of £2 to be spent on prizes for the winning boys, or a walk in the country, for which all boys assembled and marched off with the band. There was an invitation to attend the Military Tournament and a grant not exceeding £10 allowed for railway fares. The Chairman's treat of a trip to Leigh to see Colonel Cody's "Wild West Show" was a huge success and it was noted: "The boys were highly delighted, such visits to places of entertainment are red letter days in their lives." There were too, very rare excursions to Southport by train or in wagonettes, a ferryboat ride to New Brighton or a visit to the Akbar. Only dutiful boys were permitted these delights.

Access to the library was considered a treat. The boys read eagerly and handled with care copies of the "Boys' Own Paper", "Chums", the "Liverpool Echo", "Express", "Tit Bits" and books with such innocent titles as "Pleasant Reading" and "Bedford Cottages". Magic lantern and gramophone entertainments were the most common diversions and there was the occasional concert when a lady or gentleman sang a selection of respectable ballads.

Jubilee Day, Tuesday, June 22nd 1897, was probably the most exciting day of all for the boys. It was an occasion for national rejoicing to commemorate Queen Victoria's long reign and the boys bedecked the playground with red, white and blue poles and flags and marched up and down to the accompaniment of the band singing patriotic songs before freezing to attention for the National Anthem. Each boy had plum pudding and buns, and in the afternoon they all marched to Earlestown with 3d each of their mark money to spend. The festivities continued into the next day, when there was a sports day.

In later years, a fortnight's camp was arranged each year at Formby and then at Heswall, and in 1895 a school football league of four teams was formed with considerable success. The following year, the school won 17 out of 20 football matches with outside teams and for the first time the boys were examined in drawing, revealing hidden talents which won them "excellent" ratings.

After Care

The licensing and rehabilitation of lads after they left the school was an acute problem. There was little doubt that for most boys the greatest test of all was when they returned home, to the environment which had nurtured their criminality in the first instance. When times were hard and work in short supply, this particular headache for the reformers was immense. On August 26th 1895, the Superintendent sadly noted: "For some time past we have had our complement of boys and the only way I can accept new cases is by licensing boys to friends, a plan I do not approve because, if boys have no employment, they become street loafers, mix with the worst characters, and get into trouble again. For the past year and more, owing to the depression in trade, coal strikes and agricultural distress, there has not been any demand for our lads, and consequently, it has become very difficult to find places for them. I have thought it would be a good thing to ask the Home Secretary to increase our number from 150 to 170 as we have ample space for 188 boys, the Home Office requirements being 25 square feet and 300 cubic feet per boy. I have consulted the Medical Officer and he thinks the accommodation ample for 25 additional boys."

"I find also that in a number of cases the clothes given to them on leaving are soon pawned. I propose in future to give only one suit on leaving and after six months, if a lad is working steadily, to give him the second suit."

The reformers occasionally came under fire from the community. In spite of a 78½% success rate in 1899, the number of re-convictions led to a sharp public comment on the apparent shortcomings of the reformatory system. One irate man wrote to the press: "Boys who have been inmates of a Reformatory ought not to be allowed at large, when they are known to be living idle, uncontrolled and lawless lives. If one or two of the existing Institutions were set apart for such cases to be detained during their minority, the efficiency of the reformatory treatment would be more apparent."

No such rehabilitation centre was forthcoming. The Superintendent in April 1899, did make a tentative exploratory visit to the Boys' Home in St George's Street, Liverpool, to enquire their terms. He reported: "I was given to understand that the boys' earnings are taken to help support them. Should their earnings amount to over eight shillings, the excess is placed in their names in the Bank. A small sum is given to them as pocket money on special occasions, even when they do not earn sufficient to support themselves. The Home is unquestionably a boon to homeless lads, but how far it would be the answer for our lads as a home to take them out of surroundings they like but are prejudicial to their improvement, with nothing more than moral persuasion to control them and induce them to remain there, is doubtful."

The boys were supervised for three years after expiry of their sentence and the Association was required to report annually on their progress to the Home Office. 80% of the boys were from Liverpool and, when licensed, came under the supervision of the Government Inspector's Agent. The country boys were seldom visited in the early days and the Superintendent kept in touch with them by letter.

A large proportion of their time was occupied in letter writing, but a suggestion that police supervision might ease the workload was refused with the reply: "I doubt very much the wisdom of placing our boys on licence and discharge under police supervision as it would place them at a great disadvantage compared with other Schools. They are always known to the police and suspicion very often attaches to them, whereas, if they were unknown, they would not be suspected."

Such a situation in December 1900 inspired a rebuke for one Chief Constable from farm school Superintendent J Digweed: "Sir: I send you the enclosed letters received from a lad, a former inmate of this school but recently licensed. If his statements are true and there seems to be some reason to believe them, this lad has been most unjustly treated and I place the matter in your hands to prevent a repetition of such treatment. It is most difficult for our lads to obtain good places of work when they leave, and it is hard enough for them to fight the battle of life honestly and manfully without any interference of the police, but if they are to be suspected or apprehended for every offence committed in the locality in which they happen to reside, simply because they have been in a Reformatory, what chance have they to earn a living? It would be no great surprise if they should lose heart and yield to the temptation to rob to get something to eat. I feel quite sure in calling your attention to this matter that you will use your influence to put a stop to such intolerance."

Lads like Joseph were re-admitted after the Superintendent reported: "Joseph has a drunken mother, his father died when he was five and from that age he was on the streets. He was licensed six weeks ago to kindly Christian relatives and put with an uncle to engineering. The restraints of the Reformatory were irksome, he says, and he was glad to get away; the control of his uncle and the restraints of work were also irksome; he refused to work and told his uncle he wanted to do nothing."

"The uncontrolled lawless life of the streets has a charm for him and when he is free and not under supervision, he may have his way, as some others have, to the injury of other lads and loss to the public. This lad may be irreclaimable, but he ought not to be allowed to fix his own board and lodging on the community and, before a year or two, become injurious to others."

The reformers washed their hands of a boy who stole a cash box and lived with prostitutes whilst on licence. He was discharged as incorrigible.

The request of parents in 1889 for the licensing of their son Thomas to help support the family was also refused on the grounds that: "He is only a small and delicate boy and I cannot see how he could help to maintain the family if discharged. He could not in my opinion earn enough to support himself. Taking his future welfare into account, I think it would be doing injustice to the lad to allow him to leave the Institution at present."

Parents who found it hard to keep up the payments they were expected to contribute while their lads were in school often appealed for their boy to be licensed as a means of release from payment. Such a case was Albert, in 1896, who had been sent to

Reformatory boys worked as hard as the girls in their school laundry

the farm school for stealing from his blind father and being out of control. His home was comfortable but he had stayed out at nights, sleeping in outhouses and associating with bad companions. The Superintendent refused his father's request to have him home: "I think it would be prejudicial to the proper management of this school if such an application were granted for the reasons adduced by the lad's parents. I have at least eight boys whose conduct will compare more favourably with this lad and all of whom have been longer in the school and shown more diligence in their work. If he were to be licensed or discharged before such boys it would lead to discontent and absconding... The crux of the question lies in the fact that parents find it hard to keep up the payments. Release them from this and their lads might remain here for their five years admission."

Financing Reform

The Government allowance of 7/- a week towards the maintenance of a reformatory inmate was cut to 6/- in 1861, with a further reduction of 2/- when the child had been detained 3 years, providing he had reached the age of 16. The idea was threefold: 1. To force local authorities to accept some financial responsibility for the inmates from their respective areas. 2. To make the reformers even more economy-minded. 3. To guarantee that the boys and girls should not be detained in Reformatories longer than needful.

Arguments in council chambers raged fast and furiously, with the critics reasoning that private Associations undertaking the work of reformation should prove their genuine interest in that work by covering much of the expense involved. In July 1866 the Liverpool Town Council reluctantly agreed to donate 1/- a week towards the maintenance of each boy from their city, but nothing for the girls.

To maintain and instruct one of the ninety boys at the farm school in 1868 cost £19 13s 7d, 29 outfits were bought for £5 5s each and the industrial profit brought £316 2s 11d. In 1893, the Treasury allowance for maintenance at the farm school amounted to £1,859 19s 3d plus a clothing allowance of £46. Each borough and county made its own contribution of £629 5s 5d and the combined total helped considerably towards the school's outlay for that year of £2,568 6s 5d. The entire expenditure of the three schools for 1893 totted up to £8,576 7s 7d. Six years later the cost of maintenance and instruction for 125 boys was £20 10s 10d each; the cost of outfits £3 4s 4d per head on 47 boys and the industrial profit £463 2s 11d. In 1904, with 149 boys at the school, costs came to £21 6s 10d per head, with outfit expenditure of £3 16s 11d per head on 50 boys, and the industrial profit had slumped to £55 3s 10d.

Problems with Staff

The high standard of discipline and faultless behaviour required of the boys was expected also of the staff, and those who digressed could expect instant dismissal. To a teacher who enjoyed his tipple Mr Atty wrote in 1886: "You were drinking all last week and not fit for work. You were drunk when you came to work this morning. Do not come near the school until I have consulted the Vicar. If he approves, I shall advise your discharge. You have for many years now been a loss and a hindrance."

To another member of staff, late for morning duties, he penned: "I understand you have not been on duty again this morning before 7am. If I am misinformed, please see me with an explanation. If correct, I wish to know if you are unable to perform the duties allotted to you at the stated hours and if this is so, you had better place your resignation in my hand or I shall be compelled to give you formal notice."

In May 1892, the farm bailiff was dismissed for neglecting his work and disregarding orders. It was reported: "The boys are frequently left by themselves in the fields while he is at ease in his house or on visits to the village, leaving the care of the cattle and buildings to the mercy of the boys. He went off on Saturday afternoon when a pig was near farrowing, although the same pig on a previous occasion had killed all her young and eaten some of them. The boys, anxious about the stock and knowing he had gone away, sat up all night and watched her."

The job of farm bailiff was created in the ten years following the 30-year control of Mr Atty, who had included these extra duties within his function as Superintendent. It was certainly a relief to his successor when the Committee agreed that an extra man should be appointed for the job.

The farm bailiff, with a carter to help him, worked under the supervision of the Superintendent and was responsible for crop management and keeping the boys who worked on the farm "well employed". He was expected also to take a general interest in the school, to maintain discipline and devote the whole of his time to these duties. In 1900, he earned 26/6d a week. lived in a free house and bought his milk, potatoes and vegetables at wholesale prices from the school. He had 7 days holiday a year and was permitted an occasional free Bank Holiday by special permission. His wife was required to look after the poultry, for which she received 3 tons of coal a year. The boys were not allowed to milk the cows but could be instructed on a cow nearly dry, if they washed their hands before doing so. After the cows were milked and the can locked, the shippon boys carried the milk to the school.

In 1895 the cook was sent packing for being "untruthful, indecent in her conversation and too free with the boys." In the same year the teacher was dismissed after HM Inspector complained: "The school room work is not so satisfactory this year. There were twenty failures in arithmetic and there is a want of 'go' in all the work. The boys are noisy, inattentive and are not kept well at work. The teacher's indifferent, lifeless and painfully slow manner of discharging all his duties is telling badly upon the boys and the discipline of the school generally. He needs to throw more brightness and energy into his work. Half the time he seems lost in abstraction and nearly everything he does is most mechanical. The body is present but his mind is in space!"

Half a Century

By 1906, 1,833 boys had entered the school since its commencement in 1859. 44 of this number had died; 25 had been transferred; 138 found employment on farms and gardens; 779 had gone into other jobs; 450 had been discharged to family and friends; 27 enlisted; 46 emigrated; 35 absconded; 14 were sent to prison; 44 to sea and 23 had been discharged on account of disease. The total discharged was 1,625, with 208 boys under detention on December 31st 1906.

Superintendent's Letters

In those early days, the burden of writing correspondence and lengthy reports took up much of the Superintendent's time and energy. With little secretarial help, and certainly no money to spare for such a luxury, he frequently worked well into the night trying to keep pace with this demanding aspect of the job.

The Superintendent's correspondence book makes interesting reading and this story would be incomplete if some extracts were not included.

MARCH 11th 1886 - LETTER TO A LANCASHIRE FARMER
I can engage Robert to you for three months and if at that time he suits you and he is also suited, an arrangement can be made. If you board and lodge him, do his washing and give him 3/- a week, that will I think be fair. If these terms suit you I will make out his form of licence. Out of the 3/- per week you might let him have one shilling - and at the end of the term pay the balance to me and I will settle with him.

MARCH 28th 1886 - REPLYING TO A LETTER FROM THE COMMITTEE TELLING HIM OF THE DEATH BY STABBING OF A LAD LICENSED THREE YEARS PREVIOUSLY
We saw the account of the wretched end of poor Frank William, and to my limited judgement, it would seem better if he had died of Rheumatic Fever in 1882 than by knife in a drunken brawl in 1886. He had a quarrelsome temper and was prone to fight, but on the whole he was a well conducted lad and there are no punishments recorded against him.

He inherited I dare say, a tendency to drink, a tendency I fear strengthened by his home influence and surroundings and the Rheumatic fever (as I am told it often does) may have left a craving for stimulants. The Judge of all the Earth will do rights, and it is better for him to be alone with God - as one day we all must be - than to be a companion of drunkards and harlots.

We ought to shudder at the fact that in the present such dishonour and disregard of our own Heavenly Father's love is so common. I shall read your letter to the boys tonight, at our evening Service. The man who killed him is committed for trial for Wilful Murder. His relatives are all drunkens.

1911 - PERMISSION FOR A BOY TO CHANGE JOBS

Dear William. In answer to yours, I am sorry that things are not going very smoothly with you but you have had a good spell at your place. I give you permission to get a fresh place on the following conditions (1) that you get a job at better wages than you are getting - (2) that the job is on a farm or similar occupation in or near the County where you are now living - you ought now to be getting good wages and I should certainly advise you to stick to your line of work, don't be pulled into going to London as I am sure you will do better in the Country - (3) write and give me full particulars of your Employer's name, address, your work and wages as soon as you possibly can.

1911 - LETTER TO EMPLOYER WISHING TO EXCHANGE LAD

Mr J Morris. Dear Sir. I regret I have not got a suitable lad to take Jackson's place, and if I had I could not think of sending him to a place at 1/6d per week, as I seldom, if ever, place any lad at less than 3/- with board, lodging, etc. With regard to a month's notice - this I consider unreasonable for a lad in such a position, and I have instructed Jackson to leave at the end of his week's notice.

MARCH 12 1912 - TO THE COMMITTEE

I visited Jones just before Christmas - he was looking well, fat and happy and I was perfectly satisfied that he was being well looked after and had got a good home and a good situation. However, as he has raised a complaint I will visit him again at the earliest opportunity and have matters put right - I'm afraid I cannot go for a day or two as owing to the Coal Strike the train service is very bad.

1912 - LETTER TO POLICE COURT MISSIONARY

I have heard that Jackson, for whom we have been so long searching, is working for R Richards, Fishmonger, Putney St, opposite Beswick St Market, West E. I don't understand the term West E, unless he means West End. Please investigate this. When you find Jackson I want you to take the following steps. Sharply reprimand him for neglecting to report his whereabouts and particulars. Obtain his home address or place of lodging - inform him of his risk of prosecution for leaving his situation and not keeping me informed of his address. Inform him that if he writes and apologises and supplies correct addresses, I will overlook the matter and allow him to continue on Licence. Otherwise I will issue a Warrant for his apprehension. He has acted foolishly, but there is no necessity for him to dodge me or withhold the information required, if he is satisfactorily employed.

11th NOVEMBER 1913 - TO THE CHIEF CONSTABLE, DOUGLAS, I.O.M.

Sir. In reply to yours of the 7th inst. I beg to inform you that the reward of one pound is offered for the apprehension of an absconder with a view to covering the expenses incurred; but when the arrest is made by the School officials and at the expense of the School, no reward is paid. I am however extremely obliged to your Officer for the information which undoubtedly led to the arrest of Henry and although no reward is offered for "information" which may, or may not, prove of any assistance, still as this was so serviceable, I have much pleasure in enclosing a cheque for 10/- in recognition of the same. Trusting PO Ball may be allowed to have the same for his own use and also hoping this will meet with your approval.

1912 - LETTER TO GOVERNOR, HM PRISON, CANTERBURY

Sir. I much regret to hear of Harris's predicament. He was a good lad in the School, he had had no previous convictions, and his conduct in the Army since leaving the School has been good. Whilst in School his faults were mainly the outcome of stupidity and want of manliness, but never underlined of any malicious or criminal tendency. Can you explain why he was sent to the Quarter Sessions instead of being dealt with summarily? Can you oblige me with a report of his case, either newspaper or otherwise, so that I can be better acquainted with it. I should like to help the lad if possible and also try to avoid his discharge from the Army, unless there are any further circumstances prohibiting such a course.

1912 - ENQUIRY REGARDING BAND BOYS, 2nd DEVONS

Dear Sir. I am much obliged for your enquiry re Boys for Band of 2nd Devons. Unfortunately I have none about 18 years of age at present, as a rule I have several of that age and have some difficulty in getting them into Army Bands - so that later on I may be glad of another enquiry from you. However, I have two lads very anxious to get into an Army Band and I could well recommend them. I enclose particulars respecting them and shall be glad to know if there is any chance of a vacancy for them. I notice you mention sending them to Exeter for attestation. Could this not be done here at Warrington? That is the course we usually adopt. I note you cover railway expenses - would that include return fare if sent to Exeter and rejected? Attestation at Warrington would avoid that. I regret delay in answering, but as the lads were so young I have secured parents' consent before bringing their case forward.

1912 - LETTER TO PARENT

Madam. Your son Leonard will be allowed to return home on

Saturday for the purpose of obtaining employment. I will remind you that under the Childrens Act 1908, he remains under the authority and supervision of the School until he attains the age of 19 years. It is important that he should have suitable employment as soon as possible, particulars of which must be reported to me. I recognise your difficulty in obtaining such until the boy is seen by his would be employer, hence he will be allowed to come Saturday. I would further remind you that should he in any way expose himself to the danger of crime, by lounging about unemployed, or associating with known bad characters, he renders himself liable to be recalled to the School.

1912 - PRIVATE COWAN, PARKHURST, I.O.W.

Dear Cowan. I was both upset and troubled when I received your letter this morning. I am sending you the 3/6d to get you out of your present difficulty, but bear in mind, you will not receive another halfpenny piece until your term expires. It is quite evident that you are going the wrong way and I put this down to the fact that you are in with a bad lot; let me warn you; pull yourself together as you appear to me to be approaching serious trouble rather too quickly. Ever since you left here I have suspected this, as you have been trading on my good nature and begging for something in every letter you have written me; I like to receive letters from old boys, but letters like yours always make me think that there is not a decent trustworthy lad within the School or without.

Your remarks re the Army are a deliberate insult to a proven noble profession and it is such as you that drag its name in the mire. You have evidently found that the Army is no place for a shirker and I can tell you, it is a haven of rest in comparison to civil life. Candidly, I very much dislike the general tone of your letter this morning as it reeks of impertinent dissatisfaction. Why you have even dared to dictate to me what to do with my lads; what experience and what authority can you quote for such unbecoming action? As you are so dissatisfied with your present position, let me advise you to look around and see what part you have played in making things brighter, you will find nothing I dare wager. Following on my remarks about boys, I have never intentionally sent a lad out of this School to a place where I thought he would not prosper with hard, honest work and out of the hundreds that I turn out, I can safely say that some of my best results are shown in the Army. Let me advise you to take this warning seriously and in time I should like to hear from you again on this subject.

1913 - LETTER TO PARENT

Dear Madam. I am very sorry to hear of your trouble at home. We do not as a rule grant leave of absence for the purpose of attending Funerals, exceptions are sometimes made when it is the case of a father or mother, but even then a Doctor's Certificate should accompany the application. I really think that the boy will have far happier recollections of his little sister if he remembers her as she was when he was at home on leave quite recently. I trust you will be able to see this in the right light, and possibly afterwards you may realise it is the happier course as far as the boy himself is concerned.

1916 - REPORT TO COMMITTEE
Smart has been working at home which was not of the best but in the circumstances I think you will agree that it was a special case. The boy's father is totally blind and Smart has worked well and was able to keep his Father and the little ones from want.

1918 - LETTER TO PARENT
Mrs Dapper, Stratford. Dear Madam. Your son Arthur received your letter dated 5.3.1918 and I wish to point out to you that you have made many statements which are likely to cause very much unhappiness to your son and which also are most unfair. We know quite well that he should be working for you but he did wrong and there is bound to be sufferings for wrongs done. Here he has commenced afresh and the past should be buried for he must have a chance but you are constantly rubbing it into him that he should be helping at home and the old wound is kept open. Encourage him to do right, write cheery letters and then he will strive for the good instead of the bad. With regard to his fare I know that times are hard but you must agree with me that we could not possibly pay fares home. Letters received from you have all contained the statements of "working for you". Please give him a chance to do well. I shall write to you later about the Army as he particularly wishes to go and I promised to let him.

OFFENCES AND PUNISHMENT
Victorian Attitudes

A warning from the Police in 1855....
"Keep your eyes open for lads with balls and sticks in the streets. We have heard of several panes of glass being broken and various ladies being spun around by the lads in their anxiety to drive their balls the way they want them. Send them to the fields."

It was an age when Queen Victoria ruled supreme. Her magisterial authority was far-reaching and was reflected in most middle and upper class homes in an intolerance of disorder and any form of rebellion against authority.

Sir William Harcourt, a kindly and pioneering Home Secretary concerned about the hundreds of children under 14 who were being sent to reformatories in 1880 was most anxious that they should be admitted, instead, to an Industrial School for instruction. Queen Victoria regarded his merciful crusade with scepticism. In reply to his plea for some remission of sentence for a child who had committed a comparatively trivial offence, the Queen's Secretary firmly replied on her behalf: "Her Majesty was interested in all you said about the youthful criminals. She would like to whip them, but it seems that that cannot be done."

In affluent homes mischievous children were handled with a firmness which would today send NSPCC men scurrying to their doors. Impish inclinations were promptly quelled by a sound thrashing from a nanny, with a firm and unsympathetic hand. High-spirited children were locked in dark cupboards or made to stand face to wall in earnest contemplation of their naughtiness for long periods of fearful hours, whilst in country areas it was not unusual to see a small penitent human scarecrow, dutifully serving his or her punishment frightening away the birds from the orchards and fields.

The founders of charity schools for the poor were fearful of disorder as well as philanthropic. Sound instruction in the catechism and principles of the established Church was designed to produce a moral populace and education in reading, writing and arithmetic to prepare the poor to meet the two great evils which threatened to engulf them - idleness and ignorance.

The hands of any school child who misbehaved in class were tied and a placard displaying some derisory remark was fastened around his or her neck. Other miscreants received 12 strokes of the birch to coincide with 12 ticks of the school clock. At the Charity Schools in Nantwich, Cheshire, 40 boys wore blue caps to enable people to observe their behaviour abroad. The young had to work very hard on their good behaviour to be rewarded with a sugar plum!

Early Punishments

There was insignificant violence or vandalism but theft was endemic and punishment in the 1850's, which varied in severity between areas, was horrendous. In those years preceding the Reformatory Act and the first glimmer of understanding towards a better deal for the juvenile offender, children were imprisoned in the common Gaol or House of Correction with or without hard labour, for a period not exceeding three calendar months. Whippings could be ordered in addition at the whim of the magistrates, and the justices had power to impose fines of up to £3 as well as to imprison. The following table gives some examples of the severe sentences meted out, and of their inequity.

PLACE	OFFENDER	STEALING	SENTENCE
Salford	boy, 13	2 biscuits	3 mths hard labour & whipping
Salford	12 year old	2 buns	1 day's hard labour
Salford	12 year old	tape measure	1 day hard labour & whipping
Salford	11 year old	1d worth potatoes	1 day hard labour & whipping
–	14 year old	3 black puddings	2 mths hard labour (in 1857)
–	14 year old	coconut	3 months hard labour
–	2 boys	lame hen	3 months hard labour each
Burnley	John,15	3 air pistols	£1 or 1 mth hard labour(1854)

Burnley	**Mary Ann,14**	**clock**	**£1 or 1 mth hard labour(1854)**
Heaton Norris	**Rose Ann,12**	**Shambrey dress value 4/6d**	**dismissed on surety of £20 for future good behaviour**

Perhaps Rose Ann was from an affluent family - £20 was a fortune in those days and Justices Sir Ralph Pendlebury and Peter Edward Marsland seem to have been unusually lenient.

The Houses of Correction were under the direct administration of the Justices and supported by the county rates. The turnkey taskmaster under the direction of the Governor fixed the kind and quantity of work to be done by each prisoner. None was allowed to be idle. They scurried around like the mice which plagued the kitchens, sweeping, scrubbing, polishing, the routine varying only to include school lessons and lectures by the Chaplain on the error of their ways. Once a week they received a top-to-tail wash and change of linen including a cotton shirt and flannel vest, and woe betide any turnkey who observed any "unusual scratching of the head" and failed to report this to the Governor.

In addition, each area had a "whipping" policeman, appointed by the Justices for that purpose. Payments for whipping appear frequently in municipal and parish accounts from an early date. "Lancaster Court 9th February, 1856. Justices William Bolden and James Thomson agreed that John and James, both aged 12, for the theft of a small quantity of beans value 1d, be each privately whipped by James Pye of the township of Skerton, he being a fit and proper person and the Constable appointed by us the said Justices for that purpose, instead of any imprisonment or fine." A whipping was the sentence on a 12-year-old who stole two oatcakes. The lash was also used on a gang of ten boys, aged from 10 to 12, for the theft of two oranges...on a boy of 10 who stole a fowl...and others for stealing a cotton sheet...a cricket bat...a rabbit...eggs...a bottle of ale...5½d...a cap.

The birching was normally carried out in private, usually on the day the order was given. Most "birch rods" were made in prisons to standard specifications and resembled the brooms used by gardeners for sweeping up leaves. The twigs were bound together at the thick end to form a handle, and the remainder left free with the loose ends forming a spray. Those used in administering corporal punishment to boys aged between 10 and 16 weighed 9 ounces and were 40 inches in overall length, with a 15-inch handle. For boys under 10 years, there was a smaller birch weighing 6 ounces, overall length 34 inches, length of handle 8 inches, and circumference of the spray at the centre 5½ inches.

A horror story circulated widely among apprehensive youngsters was that the birch was soaked in brine before use, in order to make the punishment more painful. This was untrue. The twigs of a birch kept for some time tended to become brittle and it would be soaked in water to make it more supple and to prevent twigs from breaking during use.

The punishment was usually given in a cell or private room at a neighbouring police station or within the precincts of the court. The birch was applied across the bare buttocks, with the boy bending over a low bench or table while policemen held his hands and sometimes his feet to ensure that he did not move. Another method was for a constable to take the boy on to his back, drawing the boy's hands down over his shoulders; a colleague held the boy's feet, drawing his legs around the sides of the first constable, who then leaned forward while the birch was swished by a third. In another area a constable would bend the boy over and hold his head between his knees, while a second officer administered the birch, and in a neighbouring district the boy could be strapped to an apparatus similar to the triangle used for corporal punishment in prison. Parents or guardians rarely exercised their statutory right to attend.

Regulations required that the judicial whipping should be "sufficiently severe to cause a repetition of it to be dreaded."

Not until 1904 was the maximum penalty of 18 strokes reduced to 12, and then only in England. Some schools accepted the Home Office circular as a direct order. Others regarded it only as an expression of opinion and, in defiance of the circular, continued to exercise their full powers under the old rule in cases of necessity. They were eventually forced to conform.

With the passing of the Reformatory Act came the first substantive opportunity for the children to escape from the hopeless treadmill of poverty, illiteracy and lack of opportunity. For serious offences or the slightest trace of misbehaviour, or through "crimes" which were no fault of their own, such as vagrancy, boys and girls of tender years were put away for lengthy periods of time, serving up to five years in an effort to correct their behaviour, rehabilitate and eventually train them for citizenship. It was a system which weathered many years and although harsh, austere and unyielding for the young, it was the end of a penal regime based on terror and lack of understanding. Even so, many Reformatory School sentences carried a brief preliminary period of imprisonment until 1899, when this system was abolished after prolonged argument. The table gives a fair cross-section of offences and the sentences imposed over the years.

The similarity in the sentences for trivial and more serious offences shows how unfair the system was to the petty offender, and it was not until 1915 that shorter sentences of three years were more in evidence, with additional years for more serious offences, and depending on the number of previous convictions.

As the 1900's dawned there were still many young down-and-outs bedding down in any convenient outhouse or water closet, and it was an act of providence for them to be picked up by the police for some misdemeanour and packed off via the courts to the Reformatory Schools. For boys like 14-year-old Alex, found starving and sleeping in a stable with no visible means of subsistence, and James, aged 14 of Liverpool, who was arrested while wandering in Church Street seeking alms, five years in a

DATE	OFFENDER	OFFENCE	SENTENCE
1856	William, 14	House breaking, theft of silver, fruit knife & gold breast pin	14 days prison; 4 years reformatory
1856	boy, 13	Theft of handkerchief	30 days prison; 3 years reformatory
1856	boy, 12	Theft of handkerchief	30 days prison; 3 years reformatory
1856	boy, 13	Theft of 20lbs iron	14 days hard labour, 3 years reformatory
1857	John, 13	Theft of 2 tame pigeons, value 1/8d	21 days prison; 5 years reformatory
1857	Francis,11	Theft of 3 ducks, value 5/-	1 month prison; 5 years reformatory
1857	William, 14	Theft of 7d	14 days prison; 5 years reformatory
	Henry, 13	Theft of clothing from Whiston workhouse, where he was an inmate	21 days prison; 5 years reformatory
	George, 9	Theft of trousers, value 3/-	21 days prison; 5 years reformatory
1885	boy, 11	Attempted indecent assault on his 10-year-old playmate	6 months hard labour,6 years reformatory
	James, 12	Theft of 1/-	60 days prison & a whipping; 3 yrs reformatory
1892	Harry, 11	Theft of an overcoat	5 years reformatory (then licensed to a draper)
1893	George, 13	In possession of turnip, thought to be stolen	5 years reformatory
1893	Albert, 12	Theft of 3 coconuts, value 6d	5 years reformatory
1894	Isaac, 13	Theft of a ball, value 4d	5 years reformatory
	John, 13	Theft of 4 apples, value 2d	5 years reformatory
	Richard, 11 (Two previous convictions)	Theft of 3 apples, value 1d	5 years reformatory (licensed to a farmer after 4 years)
	James, 13; servant with 2 previous convictions	Embezzlement of 9/6d from employer	5 years reformatory (licensed 1897 to enlist in Kings Royal Regiment
	William, 13	Unlawful possession of 2 oranges	5 years reformatory
1895	Charles, 12	Theft of 18 postage stamps	5 years reformatory (licensed to a baker after 4 years for good behaviour)
1905	Fred, 12	Ill-treating a sheep by beating it with a stick	5 years reformatory
1905	William, 15	Sexual assault on girl, 13	5 years reformatory
	Jacob, 14 (a first offender)	Wilful damage worth 1/- to a wardrobe	5 years reformatory (then licensed to sea)
	James, 15	Rape of girl under 13 years	5 years reformatory

THREE REFORMATORY BOYS

Left: 12-year-old Eustace. 10 days imprisonment and 5 years Reformatory in 1892 for stealing three pigeons. One previous committal for stealing pigeons; received 10 strokes of the birch.

Below left: 14-year-old Charles. Four years in a reformatory for stealing from a shop till. "Lack of parental control" and parents "intemperate but honest". One previous committal for house-breaking.

Below: 15-year-old William. 3 years in a reformatory for throwing horseshoes at a train. Eight previous committals, imprisoned each time. "Mode of life" given as "Loafing around New Street Station, Birmingham"

Reformatory was a big opportunity. Orphan Hamilton, aged 13, was licensed to a farmer after serving his five years for wandering and sleeping in an unoccupied house; 14-year-old Ernest from London, found sleeping in the open air with no funds, was licensed to sea; Frederick, aged 15, also from London and found begging in 1910, served a four year sentence before enlisting in the Royal Marines.

As the years progressed, the variety of job opportunities for lads increased, with vacancies as apprentice blacksmiths, bleachers, gardeners, waiters, farm and mill hands, carters, pit boys, fishermen, electricians, munition workers and in 1915, vacancies for motor mechanics being offered to young offenders. Some teenagers who had earlier been rejected by parents as another hungry mouth to feed could find themselves with a warm invitation to rejoin the family circle when their sentence expired; they had a trade at their fingertips and so were endowed with earning potential. However, in an effort to give the boys and girls a fresh start away from the environmental difficulties and the bad influence of family and friends, few of the youngsters were licensed to parents.

The First World War helped to empty the Reformatories. There were lads like 13-year-old Horace with no previous convictions, who was admitted in June 1916 as a "nuisance to the neighbourhood and shopkeepers" and licensed in 1918 to an Army Band. 15-year-old Hugh was licensed to the Navy after serving a three year sentence for wilful damage by setting fire to a packing case; licensed to the Army before his five-year sentence was completed was Harry, aged 14, of Preston; and 15-year-old Harold of Halifax, who was sentenced to three years for stealing a purse containing 1½d, was licensed to the Army and later reported "killed in action". Army discipline ultimately solved the problem of a large number of children aged between 12 to 15 and reported in 1914, 1915 and 1916 as being beyond the control of their parents. After serving sentences in Reformatory Schools, the majority finished up in the Services.

The Girls

Girls who came before the Courts were in the main a pathetic lot. Old beyond their years through sharing the responsibility and grief of bringing up a large family on an empty purse, few possessed the luxury of a toy or doll. On the whole, the offences they committed, although not condonable, were an indication of their deprivation. The sight of a pretty silk handkerchief, a piece of ribbon, a new dress or shawl, a rustling petticoat and other frippery must have been a sore temptation to a ragged girl.

But purloining items of fashion carried hard penalties. For stealing a petticoat, 14-year-old Sarah received a three months' sentence with hard labour and Ann, aged 11, seven days with hard labour for the theft of a frock and cape. Lydia, aged 15, served one month's hard labour for the theft of a silk hand-

YEAR	GIRL	OFFENCE	SENTENCE	EVENTUAL FATE
1894	Elizabeth, 15	Wandering in Lime St, L'pool, begging	$3\frac{1}{2}$ yrs	1897 licensed to service (5 months early - good behaviour
	Jane*, 14	Wandering in city, begging	4 yrs	
1895	Lucy Rose*, 12	Theft of 2 pairs of boots	5 yrs	1899 lic to service (good b.)
	Emma*, 15, of Blackburn	Theft of purse, value 1/-		licensed to service but returned after 3 mths as unsatisfactory
1895	Sarah*, 15, of Wolverhampton (semi-literate)	Wandering abroad, lodging in an out-side closet, no means of subsistence, not giving a good account of herself	3 yrs	Most licensed to service
	3 girls, 14	Attempting suicide	4 yrs each	
	Margaret, 15	Theft of a skirt & 2/- from mother	4 yrs	
	Alice, 15	Common assault on her grandmother	3 yrs	
	Beatrice, 13, of Great Yarmouth	Administering the poison spirits of salts to her mother with intent to injure	5 yrs	
	Margaret, 13	Theft of $\frac{1}{2}$d	5 yrs	licensed to service
	Vera, 15, of Derby	Refusing to obey workhouse officials while a pauper inmate	4 yrs	
	Alice, 15	Being a bad influence at Lichfield Industrial School	3 yrs	
	Emily, 12, of Hull	Theft of girl's dress	5 yrs	1917 licensed as ward maid at a hospital
	Lily, 15,	Theft of pair of gaiters	4 yrs	Became a factory hand
1914	Esther, 15	Theft of food, value 13/5d	3 yrs	Became shop assistant
	Hannah, 14	Theft of 2 fowls		Became a laundress
1914	Annie, 15	Theft of 7/6d from parents	3 yrs	Licensed to service
	Elizabeth, 14	Theft of 2/- from mother	5 yrs	
	May, 15	Theft of sheets, value 2/3d	4 yrs	Died of influenza
1916	Olive, 13	Theft of 2/-	5 yrs	Died of influenza
1919	Frances, 16	Theft of bicycle	3 yrs	
1920	Irene, 15	Theft of bunch of flowers	3 yrs	
	Johannah, 15, of Sunderland	Shopbreaking and theft of boots, shoes, coats & 12 blouses, value £22 16s	4 yrs	
1920	Alice, 14	Theft from children in streets	4 yrs	
1920	Margaret, 14	Theft of 32/0 from her stepmother	5 yrs	

kerchief and Margaret, the same age, three months for stealing a gold watch and one earring. Two others were imprisoned for six months each for stealing a dress and a parasol. Three weeks before Christmas in 1856, 13-year-old Margaret was sent to prison by Prescot Justices for stealing a boy's suit. She got 21 days' hard labour and afterwards five years in a reformatory.

The girls who arrived in Liverpool under police escort to serve their time in the Mount Vernon Green Reformatory came from as far away as Carlisle, Leicester, Knaresborough, Bedford, Leeds and London. As with the boys, their Reformatory School sentences seemed painfully severe for the majority of offences and there was the same failure to discriminate between serious and petty offenders. But they did get a three to five year stay in a place of safety and sustenance, with the opportunity of learning to read and write, to behave with mannerly correction and God-fearing respect; and eventually to become proficient in all aspects of housecraft. The "successes" emerged as clean, efficient, trustworthy and biddable servant girls, to be packed off into service with selected families. The table shows the apparent arbitrariness of the sentences and the gradual opening of more job opportunities for women after the turn of the century. There is an example of a child living rough as late as 1912 (Sarah of Bristol) and several of theft from within the family, showing that parents were not slow to bring their offending offspring to court. Those marked (*) were noted as having only one parent. Two instances of deaths in the Reformatory School are included and one case of a girl discharged to a workhouse because she was chronically ill.

Changes in the Law

With the establishment of the Probation of Offenders Act 1907, more options became available for the handling of young offenders. The idea of giving delinquents a second chance by putting them under the supervision of a counsellor and friend in the person of a probation officer, but at the same time warning them of the consequences of another offence, had its appeal to some Justices. However, there were still those who continued to believe in a strong line of retribution.

In November 1916 Arthur, aged 14, was sent to Borstal for four years, Borstal detention, introduced in 1908, was organised on military lines and operated within former prisons, with heavy emphasis on custodial and disciplinary aspects. Arthur's offence? Travelling on the railway without paying his fare.

The regulations were still in force up to 1938, with the courts in Scotland exercising power to order a whipping on summary conviction for a wide range of common law offences committed by boys under the age of 16.

In 1900, 3,385 birchings of young offenders took place in England and Wales. By 1936 the figure had decreased to 166 in spite of the growth in the number of young offenders being brought before the courts. In the Children and Young Persons Act, 1933, Parliament had expressly directed Juvenile Courts to concentrate their attention primarily on the element of reform. By that time, there were other methods available to the court, probation being especially favoured as a means of dealing with the young delinquent. In 1935 out of 25,442 juveniles in England and Wales found guilty of indictable offences, 12,930 were placed on probation and only 218 were ordered to be birched.

The days of the thrashing policemen ended officially in 1948 when, under the Criminal Justices Act, Section 2, the sentence of whipping was abolished completely in England, Wales and Scotland.

There are few nationwide statistics available on the success or otherwise of corporal punishment. But limited statistics revealed that in one town, out of 100 boys birched before 1936, only 29 had made no subsequent appearance in the courts. Eight had later been found guilty of minor offences only, but the other 63 reappeared on more serious charges. In another town, out of 70 boys birched in 1935, 19 had made subsequent court appearances. In one town in Scotland, out of 133 boys birched during 1934 and 1935, 48 (or 36%) had subsequently been charged with further offences.

Today, youth custody has replaced Borstal. Lads cannot be thrashed and the flogging of adult male prisoners has been outlawed. The caning of boys in community homes is being phased out.

The Juvenile Court was first introduced by the Children Act of 1908, and was subsequently regulated by the Children and Young Persons Act of 1933 to deal with all youngsters between the ages of 8 and 17, with Approved Schools taking the place of the old Reformatories. Red Bank School, Newton-le-Willows, is one of the few remaining with roots which can be traced back to an original Reformatory School.

Heswall Nautical School

That there was felt to be a continued need for powerful discipline, direction and a degree of intimidation is illustrated in the entries which appear in the Heswall Nautical School Punishment Book for the years 1947-1955 (see table). Corporal punishment was still being used freely by instructors as practical instruction in the difference between right and wrong.

OFFENCE	**SENTENCE**
Not wearing bootlaces	3 cuts
Using a circular saw without permission	6 cuts across seat of trousers
Slanderous talk about 2 officers	6 cuts
Breaking bounds to meet girls in village	6 cuts
Foul language & insolence to officers	6 cuts

Offence	Punishment
Dodging work	6 cuts, loss of privileges & extra weekend work
Theft of 3 loaves from bread van, day before sailing	6 cuts, reduced to 4th class & loss of ship
Theft of potatoes	6 cuts
In possession of obscene photographs	6 cuts
Threatening boy for cigarette	6 cuts
Unfair fighting	6 cuts
Indecent doodling	6 cuts & loss of 1 week's merit money
Urinating in drill hall	6 cuts
Overstaying Easter leave & picked up by Chief in girl's flat in Manchester	6 cuts & reduced to 4th class
Hiding in gym horse preparatory to absconding	11 cuts, loss of time, delay of 1st stripe and tight probation
Using another boy's towel	6 cuts
Buying a cake from a van	6 cuts
Fouling his bed and concealing it	6 cuts
Inattention in class	6 cuts
Absconding from Christmas Leave	8 cuts, segregated at meals, loss of existing time, ordered to scrub out office, warned that it would be "Borstal next"
Whistling at girls on route march	8 cuts & delay of 1st stripe for 1 month
Insolence to an instructor	8 cuts
Theft from a motor car	8 cuts

Other methods of punishment reflected a degree of subtlety. 'Dodging about on cleaning party in billiards room - scrub out after supper Friday and Saturday; Dodging Seamanship - clean ship's bell tonight; Theft of garden produce - diet for one week; Making a trunk call on school phone without permission - fined 1/6d, the price of the call. Asleep outside bandroom - two hours' drill; theft of 20 cigarettes in village and consistently lying - loss of first stripe and to repay tobacconist price of cigarettes; Showering before 16.30 - to clean out main latrine; Attempting to break into Roman Catholic poor box during confession - loss of wo weeks' mark money, one week's money to be given to Priest.

Points of View

In our present crime-troubled society, arguments continue to rage fast and furiously as to the effectiveness of corporal punishment in keeping delinquents and hooligans under control, or as a last-ditch means of bringing to order an unruly element. On the one hand we have those who would agree totally with the eighteenth century's outstanding reformer, Jeremy Bentham, when he said, "Punishment is elevated to the first rank of benefits when it is regarded, not as an act of wrath or vengeance against a guilty or unfortunate individual who has given way to mischievous inclinations, but as an indispensable sacrifice to the common safety"; or the parents who complained to the European Court of Human Rights that corporal punishment in schools is a barbaric relic of bygone days, "humiliating, degrading and institutional violence, poisoning children's respect for freedom and violating human rights," and were rewarded for their efforts by the controversial ruling of the Court that children must not be beaten at school against their parents' wishes. Others still regard such punishment as a source of security for us all and would gladly pay towards a birch rod.

How effective was the punishment doled out in the early years, according to those who suffered it? Some years ago, a 98-year-old former Akbar lad entered into a heated correspondence in a local newspaper on the desirability of harsher punishment for young thugs. He wrote: "I was sent to the Akbar at the age of 15 for stealing and was quickly made aware of its tough discipline. One day I cheeked an officer badly and the Captain, awarding me 15 strokes of the birch, told the man known as the Punishment Corporal - 'See that you give this rascal a sound flogging'. Having seen the ship's carpenter making the long whippy rods from supplies of fresh green well-budded birch switches brought aboard every so often, I quaked."

"All the boys paraded on the quarterdeck, where the flogging-horse had been put out. I was stretched across it, with my legs and arms tied with canvas straps so that I couldn't move and my duck pants were pulled down. Then the Corporal, taking his time, birched me on my bare buttocks, swishing me with all the vigour he could muster, I clenched my teeth and tried not to squeal, but at the third stroke I let out an ear-splitting yell. It was like nothing I had ever experienced - my weals burned and stung like fire and I howled unashamedly."

"When they released me from the horse, my bottom, cut and bleeding all over from the birch strokes, was like a white-hot ball of fire and I stood in front of the ship's company, weeping and squirming with the pain and humiliation."

"After a few weeks my scars disappeared and I was none the worse for being flogged. Indeed, the Akbar taught me self-respect and made a new boy of me. I have only praise for the officers - even the Corporal, who was a kindly man, but with a stern sense of duty."

"Training ships like this are what young hooligans need today. A caning outside the trousers, though unpleasant, didn't worry us too much, but a birching on the bare skin was something we greatly feared - it really hurt."

My last word must go to 90-year-old Mrs Eileen Moir of Wallasey, whose late father was bandmaster and hospital attendant on the Akbar. She wrote to me, "The boys in those days who were termed naughty seemed to do so very little to what boys do today."